Martin R. Phillips

MYTHOLOGY

Hill Tech Ventures Inc.
Publishing Division | Nanaimo, Canada
Printed in the United States

MYTHOLOGY

Discover the Ancient Secrets of

the Greeks, Egyptians, and the

Norse

MARTIN R. PHILLIPS

ABOUT THE AUTHOR

MARTIN R. PHILLIPS

 Martin R. Phillips is an extremely passionate historian, archaeologist, and most recently a writer. Ever since Martin was a young boy he has been fascinated with ancient cultures and civilizations.

In 1990, Martin graduated with distinction from the University of Cambridge with a double major in History and Archaeology. Upon graduation, Martin worked as an archeologist and travelled the world working in various excavation sites. Over the years, while working as an archaeologist, Martin became very well cultured and gained great insights into some of the most historic civilizations to ever exist. This first hand insight into the ancient cultures of the world is what sparked Martin's newest passion, history writing and story telling.

In 2012, Martin decided to retire from archeology to focus on writing. Over the years he has seen and experienced a great deal of fascinating things from all over world. Martin now spends the majority of his free time putting all of his research, experience, and thoughts onto paper in an attempt to share his knowledge of the ancient cultures with the world.

Over the past few years Martin has excelled in his writings. His narrative style has a way of combining the cold hard facts with a story teller's intrigue which makes for an excellent reading experience.

"Live your life to the fullest and enjoy the journey!"

- Martin R. Phillips

Martin R. Phillips

PART 1

GREEK MYTHOLOGY

PART 2

EGYPTIAN MYTHOLOGY

PART 3

NORSE MYTHOLOGY

PART 1
GREEK
MYTHOLOGY

Ancient Secrets of the Greeks

INTRODUCTION

One of the most interesting aspects of the ancient Greeks is their mythology. Although only a small handful of people still believe the myths to be true, what remains is that Greek mythology fascinates us in a way that is almost incomparable to other ancient systems of belief.

Culture has yet to turn away from the mythology of the ancient Greeks, and this fact can be seen in various aspects of our modern life. Through various forms of entertainment, we come across themes and events depicted in Homer's works of the Iliad and Odyssey. We find ourselves viewing and referencing the strength and trials of Heracles. We even find various parallels between the lives and myths of the ancient Greeks to our own modern world.

The history of Greece herself cannot be separated by the mythology of its ancient peoples. From heroes such as Heracles and Perseus, to the underhanded dealings of gods and mortals alike, their story is one a creative attempt to understand the forces which dwell about us and within us.

In this book you will find specific stories central to Greek mythology. This is a key into understanding the mindset, not only of these ancient peoples, but of our modern world as well. We may not subscribe as the Greeks did to these myths as factual accounts of historical events, however, these tales allegorically represent the things that humankind still endures and rejoices in.

In this text, you will find the spirit of love, of nature, of war and of peace. These myths often deal with very blunt subject matter, as they were the dominant lens through which the world was viewed during much of ancient Greece.

The research and writing involved in bringing you this collection of Greek mythology has been an absolute pleasure, and I hope that you are as fascinated in reading this as I was in putting it together.

CHAPTER 1

In the Beginning, There was Chaos

In this chapter, we will be discussing the origin of the universe according to Greek mythology and the generations of the primordial gods, the Titans, and the Olympians.

According to Greek mythology, the universe began as an abyss. There was no matter, no light, no life or consciousness outside of this primordial chasm. Yet it was out of this very void, known as Chaos (or Khaos) that not only the Titans and later the gods of Olympus were sprung, but existence itself.

It was from Chaos that Gaia (or Gaea, "mother earth") was formed. Along with Gaia, Tartarus (the abyss, often described as a vast cave-like space beneath the earth, comparable to hell in Judeo-Christian belief), Eros (desire/biological imperative; some myths include him as a primordial god, while others claim him as a child of Aphrodite) Erebus (darkness) and Nyx (the night) were also spawned of Chaos. While other beings that would represent other necessary factors for life as we know it were later formed by Gaia and her ilk, the initial building blocks of reality were spawned directly from Chaos.

The Chaos mythos in ancient Greek religion is an interesting one. Although the myths were around long before them, two poets were the earliest sources of known, written accounts dealing with the religion of ancient Greece. Those two men were Homer and Hesiod.

Homer is best known for his two epics Iliad and Odyssey which deal largely with the Trojan wars; wars that up until more recently were considered to be a complete fabrication. It's not within the scope of this book to delve too deeply into the purported Trojan wars themselves outside of the later chapter regarding Homer's works; however, reference to these epics form much of the basis of our understanding of Greek mythological belief.

Hesiod is also best known for two epic poems, Theogony and Works and Days. It is with Theogony that this text is primarily concerned, as it delves into the mythological creation and formation of all that exists, along with the Olympian gods, their progenitors and progenies.

At the earliest times within the Greek creation myth, there was, as yet, no male presence. Gaia took it upon herself to rectify this by birthing Uranus. Gaia produced other children asexually, they were: Ourea (mountains) and Pontus (sea). Thus completes the basic structure of the planet as the Greeks would view it.

Gaia bore many other children however. With her son Uranus, she bore the Hecatonchires (indomitable giants with a hundred hands), the Titans (a powerful race of deities with whom the next chapter is primarily concerned), the Cyclopes (more commonly Cyclops; one-eyed giants) and Echidna (often known as the mother of all monsters).

With Tartarus, she conceived and gave birth to her final son Typhon. Typhon was a dragon with a hundred heads, considered the most deadly of all monsters, and in some traditions, considered the father of all monsters.

Other primordial gods produced their own offspring which covered much of life's experience. Erebus and Nyx generated Aether (the heavens, also the air which the gods breathed) and Hemera (day). On her own, Nyx generated many descendants. These were Apate (deception), Eris (discord), Geras (maturation, or aging), Hypnos (sleep), the Keres (eaters of the dead or wounded on the battlefield), the Moirai (the fates), Momus (blame or denunciation), Moros (doom), Nemesis (revenge or retribution), Oizys (suffering), Oneiroi (Dreams), Philotes (affection) and Thanatos (death).

Uranus also produced his own children, although this was not by choice. His children were purportedly spawned when Cronos {one of the principle Titans} castrated Uranus. The blood that had spilled would go on to create the Erinyes (the furies, female deities of vengeance), the Giants (aggressive and strong beings, although not necessarily larger than human), the Meliae (ash tree nymphs). Also, when the severed genitals of Uranus washed ashore, Aphrodite (the goddess of love among other things) came into being among the sea foam.

While there are many other gods in the Greek pantheon, the present list is intended to show the first few emanations of Greek deities from Chaos to Aphrodite. Other gods, their children, consorts, etc. will be referenced in later chapters.

It is interesting to note that while Greek mythology was unique in many ways, there are common threads throughout many of the world's religions. For instance, in the belief of Judaism and its descendants Christianity and Islam, at the time of creation, the world was without form and [was] void. The formation came through god's will. Although these religions are monotheistic (belief in one god) as opposed to the polytheistic (belief in multiple gods) religion of the ancient Greeks, the story of creation has its similarities. The primary difference being that where the Greeks saw many emanations of gods that created existence, in the monotheistic religion, this was carried out by one god alone.

Other religions with similarities are the Babylonian where the earth began as a dark, watery chaos; the Hindu cosmology, the universe began as empty and dark. Even Norse mythology has its origin story begin in chaos.

It is hardly difficult to realize that in order to have an account of creation, there has to be something before creation. Even the scientific theory of the big bang has the universe composed with all matter in an infinitely small point; outside of this was nothingness (which could be called chaos).

Martin R. Phillips

CHAPTER 2

The Titans' Rule

The story of the rise of the Titans begins with the god of the sky, Uranus. Uranus (the sky) and Gaia (the earth) were spouses, lovers and, together, parented the Hecatonchires, the Cyclopes, the Echidna and the Titans.

Uranus and Gaia's love affair was the stuff of legend (forgive the pun.) Uranus so loved Gaia that at night, he embraced her on all sides, mating with her. He was a devoted spouse, but was obsessed with power.

While Uranus was affectionate toward Gaia, and favored those that he would come to call Titans, he feared and despised the Hecatonchires, the Giants and the Cyclopes. He imprisoned them all in Tartarus, deep within Gaia.

The imprisonment of her children caused Gaia great pain emotionally and physically. In order to reap vengeance on her consort Uranus for what he had done to her and her children, Gaia fashioned a sickle made of flint and approached her Titan children for help. The plan was to castrate Uranus.

None of the Titans were willing to risk a confrontation with Uranus with the exception of the youngest and the most ambitious Titan. His name was Cronus.

Cronus took the sickle and laid in wait for his father to arrive. When Uranus came, Cronus ambushed him and succeeded in castrating him. Cronus cast the severed genitals into the sea, the blood of which would create the giants, the meliae and the erinyes. When the genitals washed up to shore, Aphrodite was created.

Uranus cursed his children and called them Titanes theoi, or "straining gods." There are differing legends on what happened to the sickle at this point. Some claimed that the sickle was buried in Sicily. Others would claim that the sickle had been cast into the sea. One Greek historian claimed to have found the sickle at Corcyra.

With Uranus out of the picture as ruler, Cronus came to power. Although his mother Gaia had intended for her other children, the Cyclopes and the hundred-handed ones to be released from their captivity, Cronus left them prisoners inside Tartarus. Along with them, he also imprisoned the giants. Having now angered both of his parents, Gaia and Uranus prophesied that Cronus would be himself overthrown by one of his children.

Cronus had married his sister Rhea and, fearing the prophecy of the earth and the sky, he took upon himself a desperate plan to preserve his power. When Rhea began to bear children, Cronus immediately devoured them. Although his children were immortal like him, they would, in their turn, be imprisoned within his belly.

Each of his children, the first of those who would come to be the gods of Olympus, were devoured by Cronus in this manner with the exception of the youngest child. Rhea was fed up with Cronus's actions and when she was about to bear her sixth and final child, she hid away and, once her child was born, she hid him in a cave on Mount Ida in Crete. This child's name was Zeus.

Knowing that Cronus would insist upon devouring the child, Rhea took a stone and wrapped it in swaddling clothes. Cronus devoured the stone, thinking it to be his child.

Despite Cronus's treatment of his children, the time during the rule of Cronus and Rhea was referred to as The Golden Age of the Gods. The earth was devoid of immorality. The inhabitants of the earth were moral on their own, and so did not require laws to keep them in line. This was before the existence of humankind.

There are different myths as to how Zeus was raised. One has him being raised by Gaia herself. Another has him being raised by a nymph named Adamanthea who, in order to protect the child, suspended him from a tree between the sky, the sea, and the earth, therefore keeping him just outside his father's kingdom and therefore outside of his perception. Another myth has Zeus being raised by a shepherd family in exchange for the protection of their flocks. In another telling, he was raised by a different nymph named Cynosura. In this myth, Zeus's gratitude would lead him to place Cynosura among the stars.

Yet another, and one of the more popular myths of the time, has Zeus being raised by a goat. His cries are said to have been covered by a group of armored dancers who would bang their shields together, shout and clap in order to mask the child's cries, thus keeping him outside the knowledge of Cronus.

Regardless the differing myths associated with his infancy, Zeus grew to become very powerful. When he reached manhood, he was set on overthrowing his father Cronus, and releasing his siblings from within the ruler's body. He met with Metis, a Titan of deep knowledge and wisdom. She gave him an emetic (a substance which causes one to purge) potion to give to his father.

According to one myth, Zeus slipped the concoction into Cronus's nightly drink of mead. Upon drinking the mixture, Cronus began to grow violently ill. He first vomited up the stone which he had thought to be Zeus, and then the children whom he had eaten. These children of Cronus and Rhea were quick to ally themselves with Zeus. They were Demeter, Hades, Hera, Hestia and Poseidon.

What followed is often referred to as the Titanomachy or War of the Titans. This conflict between the Titans on Mount Othrys, and the children of Cronus from Mount Olympus would last for ten years. Zeus, in search of more allies against the Titans travelled deep into Gaia to Tartarus and freed the Hecatonchires, the Giants and the Cyclopes. In gratitude for their release, the Cyclopes forged thunder and lightning and gave them to Zeus.

The Olympians would face nearly all of the Titans in this war with the exception of Themis and her son Prometheus; these two allied themselves with Zeus.

With his new allies and powers, the Olympians would defeat the Titans. Upon victory, Zeus imprisoned the Titans in Tartarus as Uranus and Cronus had imprisoned the Hecatonchires and the Cyclopes.

Zeus forced Atlas, one of the leaders of the Titan army, to hold up Uranus at the western edge of Gaia by his shoulders in order to prevent the mating of the two, and the possibility of further Titan births. It's commonly thought that Atlas was forced to hold up the earth, and is often pictured as supporting the globe on his back. However, this is a more modern interpretation, and the actual myth was that of separating Uranus and Gaia.

The Titan rule had come to an end, and the rule of Olympus had started.

CHAPTER 3

The Olympian Rule

Although which gods are included in the list of twelve Olympians varies, this number would be a constant of the major inhabitants of Olympus. Here it becomes useful to give an account of the major Olympian gods, their importance and their attributions. As the various consorts of these deities could fill up a book on their own, they will only be referenced in cases of particular importance.

Aphrodite was, as stated above, born from the sea foam after Cronus's genitals were cast into the sea. She was the goddess of love and beauty. She was among the gods invited to the wedding of Peleus and Thetis who would become the parents of the legendary Achilles. It was said that the only goddess not to be invited to the wedding was Eris, the goddess of discord.

When Eris showed up anyway, true to her nature, she tossed a golden apple into the center of the other goddesses inscribed with the words, "to the fairest."

Three of the goddesses immediately claimed that the gift was theirs by right of their beauty. These were Aphrodite, Hera and Athena.

When the three could not come to a decision regarding ownership of the golden apple, each thinking themselves to be the fairest of the goddesses, they brought the matter before Zeus. Wanting to avoid the quarrel, Zeus passed the decision onto Paris of Troy.

Paris was the son of the Trojan King Priam. The goddesses washed themselves in the spring of Mount Ida and went before Paris for his decision. They rent their clothing and asked him to judge. Although having been given permission to set his own conditions by Zeus, he could not decide among them as he found them all to be supremely beautiful.

The goddesses, undaunted by his inability to decide between them began offering him various things in exchange for his declaration of who was the fairest. Athena offered him wisdom, courage, and glory in battle; Hera offered control of Europe and Asia; but it was Aphrodite whose offer he accepted. Her offer was to grant him a wife who was more beautiful than all of the women of the earth.

The problem with Aphrodite's offer was that this woman was already married to a Spartan king named Menelaus. Undaunted, Paris abducted his new goddess-given bride, a woman named Helen out from under Menelaus. The legend goes that the other two goddesses, scorned Aphrodite and Paris for this, and they would go on to initiate the Trojan War, of which Homer's Iliad is largely concerned.

Apollo was the god of the sun, of light, of truth, and poetry among other things. He was often depicted as bearing a bow and arrow, or often a lyre. He was the son of Zeus and Leto, a daughter of Coeus and Phoebe (Titans), and twin brother to Artemis. Due to Hera's anger and jealousy of Leto as her husband had lain with her and the two produced offspring, Apollo's early life was largely occupied by protecting his mother against Hera's wrath.

Hera's first attempt on Leto was by sending Python, a dragon who dwelled beneath the living surface of Gaia. In order to be equipped to protect his mother, Apollo entreated Hephaestus to provide him with armaments. He received his iconic bow and arrow and, at only four days old, Apollo was said to have slain Python.

Hera wasn't done going after Leto, however. Her next attempt on Leto was commenced by sending the giant Tityos to dispatch her rival. Tityos was around twenty two square miles' worth of giant but, with the help of his sister Artemis, Tityos was defeated and cast into Tartarus by Zeus. While in Tartarus, Tityos was doomed to have his liver perpetually consumed by vultures.

Although he was considered a healer of man and god in Greek mythology, he also could bring death and disease with his arrows. One notable instance of this began with a simple insult.

Niobe was the wife of Amphion, one of the founders of Thebes and its ruler. She boasted to Leto that she had seven times as many children (seven sons and seven daughters) as Leto's two: Apollo and Artemis. Apollo and Artemis swiftly killed all (or in some versions, all but one) of Niobe's children; Apollo killed the sons while Artemis killed the daughters.

Apollo was bisexual and had a vast number of male and female consorts. He bore many children, however er the story of Apollo and Daphne is one of the most famous. As the story goes, Apollo was remarking to Eros that his bow and arrow were above his station, that he was unfit to wield them.

Eros, having had enough of Apollo's taunts shot two arrows: A golden arrow of love through Apollo's heart and a leaden arrow of hate or disgust into the nymph Daphne. Apollo immediately pursued the nymph who was disgusted and fled his advances. She entreated her father Peneus, the river god to help her. Her father turned her into a laurel tree, but Apollo's love of her was unwavering. He embraced the branches, but even they shrank away from him. He declared that as he retained eternal youth, so should the leaves of the tree never decay. He would guard the tree from any who would do it harm, and use its branches as crowns for the leaders of the world.

Ares was the god of war. A son of Zeus and Hera (one of Zeus's rare dalliances with his own wife), Ares took his sister Enyo (goddess of destruction) as his consort. He was the father of Phobos (fear) and Deimos (terror) borne from Aphrodite. According to Homer, Ares was despised by his father Zeus for his lust for war.

While he was immortal, and loved nothing more than warfare, he was highly intolerant of pain. In Homer's Iliad, Ares was injured in the battlefield of Troy, and his cries were heard throughout the world. He went back to Olympus whining to his father Zeus to heal him. Zeus quickly let Ares know how much he was despised but, as Ares was his son, he did in fact heal him.

Ares is said to have always gone into war with Enyo joining him on his chariot, and this chariot was driven by Phobos and Deimos.

Artemis, twin of Apollo, was the goddess of the hunt, the moon, the forests and the hills. She was the first of the twins to be born, and actually acted as midwife to her mother Leto during Apollo's birth. Her weapon was, like that of her brother, the bow.

Artemis believed her destiny to be as a midwife, and unlike many of the philandering gods, she remained a virgin. All of her companions were also virgins and, one day as they were bathing, a man named Actaeon came upon them. He was hunting with his hounds at the time, but was struck by the beauty of Artemis and her cohorts and stopped to gaze upon them further.

When Artemis discovered the man peeping at herself and her companions, she became furious and turned him into a stag. His hunting dogs, no longer recognizing their master tore him to pieces.

Artemis was certainly not one to be trifled with. When Agamemnon, one of the legendary warriors of the Trojan War in Iliad, offended Artemis, she exacted her vengeance by calming the winds which bore Agamemnon's fleet toward Troy. Stranded in the middle of the sea, Agamemnon's only choice to appease Artemis was to offer up his daughter Iphigenia.

There are differing accounts as to what exactly happened when Artemis came upon Iphigenia. Some myths say that Artemis spared the woman because of her bravery, others say that Iphigenia was taken as a priestess to help worshippers offer sacrifice to the goddess, while still others say that Athena did in fact take Iphigenia as sacrifice.

Athena was the goddess of wisdom, intelligence, crafts, and architecture and was the patron goddess of Athens which bears her name. Athena's birth is as interesting as any other myths about her. She was borne of the goddess Metis.

Metis was the goddess of wisdom and craftiness. Zeus and Metis became entangled in a romantic tryst but, fearing a prophecy which stated that Zeus's offspring by Metis would come to be more powerful than Zeus himself, he consumed Metis (in some versions, he turned her into a fly first) as his father Cronus had done with his Olympian children.

His efforts were too late, however, as Metis was already pregnant with Athena. Metis would give birth in Zeus's belly, and she forged weapons and armor for her new daughter. Athena grew to adulthood and split the head of Zeus, springing forth from within armed and grown. Zeus, despite the manner of Athena's technical birth, came through the encounter unscathed.

Other traditions do exist where Athena was born as the mind of god. She still sprung from his forehead, but as a result of his intention of creating another world by use of the word logos.

Among her other attributions was that she was a patron of heroes. In Homer's Odyssey, she is impressed by the hero Odysseus as he tries to make his way toward his home of Ithaca. She could only assist him from afar, however, by implanting thoughts into his head on his travel back to his homeland.

Demeter was the goddess of the harvest. Of all the cults in ancient Greece, the cults of Demeter were possibly the most widespread and definitely the most secretive.

As the story of Demeter and Persephone is detailed in the book Ancient Greece of this series, it seems fitting to give a different account of the goddess's myth.

During her search for Persephone, Demeter took the form of an elderly mortal woman and called herself Doso. She was found by four daughters of the king of Eleusis, a man named Celeus. She claimed that she had been attacked by pirates, and entreated them to help her find work befitting an old woman.

Demeter asked the king for shelter, which he gave. He asked if she could nurse his children Triptolemus and Demophon. Demeter did the king one better. Due to his kindness and hospitality, she secretly began feeding Demophon ambrosia (the food of the gods), a substance which would grant immortality to those who partook of it. Then at night, she would hold the boy in the fire to cleanse him of his mortality.

When the queen of Eleusis, Celeus's wife Metanira stumbled across the scene, she took the situation at face value and screamed. Demeter abandoned her quest to make the boy immortal, and instead taught his brother the secrets of planting, harvesting and agriculture. This is, according to Greek mythology, how the people of the earth learned to grow crops.

Dionysus was the god of wine and merriment. He was born of a mortal woman named Semele. Hera, usually quick to discover her husband's infidelities, went to Semele as a nurse, or an old woman. Semele told the disguised goddess of the unborn child's father, that it was Zeus's child.

Hera encouraged Semele to doubt the Olympian heritage of her unborn child. Semele then went before the disguised Zeus and demanded that he reveal himself. When she persisted, he reluctantly agreed and showed himself in all of his glory. As an unconcealed god, the mortal woman could not survive the sight, and she died in flame.

Zeus, not wanting his child to also perish, removed the still developing child Dionysus from his dead mother's womb. To allow the boy to grow to full infancy, Zeus sewed Dionysus into his thigh. After a few months of incubation, Dionysus was born. Thus, he was a twice-born god, once of his mother Semele and once from the thigh of Zeus himself.

In another popular Dionysian tale, Silenus, Dionysus's foster father had passed out in the rose garden of a king. The king nursed him back to health for ten days. On the eleventh day, Silenus took the king to Dionysus who, being so grateful for Silenus's return and the hospitality of the king, offered the latter his choice of any reward that he so chose.

The king's name was Midas.

Hades was the god of the underworld. Despite modern depictions, Hades was not the most reviled of all the gods. In fact, during the Titanomachy, he fought bravely with the Olympians against their Titan foes. He was the oldest male childe of Cronus and Rhea and was therefore the last to be regurgitated by the former. This being the case, he can also technically be considered the youngest male (Hestia being the oldest {and youngest} of all the children).

While there was a later belief that Hades and Dionysus were one and the same, the people feared Hades. They would sacrifice black animals such as sheep to the underworld god and, as it was believed that the blood dripped through a crack in the earth, would avert their faces to avoid seeing him.

Hades took Persephone as his wife, but when Demeter refused to allow the crops of the earth to grow, she was returned for two-thirds of the year.

His chariot was led by four black horses, and he kept as a pet and guardian the three headed dog Cerberus.

Hephaestus, the god of fire, masonry and metal working, was the only one of the gods who was considered to be ugly. Born of Zeus and Hera, he often took his mother's side. In a particular argument of the espoused gods, Hephaestus stepped in between them. Zeus, furious at Hephaestus's intervention cast him out of Olympus, throwing him by the leg.

Hephaestus flew for the space of a full day, finally landing with an enormous impact on the island of Lemnos. He was nursed back to health, but would always walk with a limp. (although another version has Hera casting him out because he already had a withered foot.)

Despite being cast out, Hephaestus was able to regain his place on Olympus.

In order to prevent the other gods from fighting over who would be able to marry Aphrodite, Zeus arranged the marriage between the goddess of beauty and Hephaestus. Although he was considered to be the most balanced of the gods, the insatiable Aphrodite was constantly unfaithful.

Although she was married to Hephaestus, Aphrodite had a long-running romance with Ares. The two were spotted one day by Helios (the charioteer of the sun), who quickly made Hephaestus aware of the situation.

Rather than confront them outright, Hephaestus set a trap. He forged a net which was so fine it could not be seen by the naked eye. He set his trap and waited for its prey.

When Ares and Aphrodite were ensnared, Hephaestus brought forth the two naked gods to shame them before the others on Olympus. The other gods, however, only laughed at the sight. It wasn't until Poseidon persuaded Hephaestus to release the two by promising that Ares would pay the fine of the adulterer, that of returning the wife and reclaiming the price he had paid as dowry to Zeus.

Aphrodite not only laid with Hephaestus's brother Ares, but a prodigious string of gods and men. Hephaestus was hardly a pitiable cuckold though, as he fathered many children and had many consorts of his own.

Hephaestus worked the forges both on Olympus, and within the volcanos of the earth. To help him walk, he forged two robots out of metal (not joking) and endowed them with the gift of artificial intelligence. These two robots would serve as highly intelligent crutches to the god.

Hera was the queen of the Olympian gods, and goddess of marriage, birth and women. Her symbol was the peacock, and these birds were said to have drawn her chariot.

Much of the stories regarding Hera are in regard to her vengeance upon the women with whom her husband Zeus engaged in sexual intercourse, and her wrath against the children born of these affairs.

One of the most amusing stories about Hera and her infamous temper regards a man named Tiresias. When he was young, he came across the sight of two mating snakes, and struck them with a stick. His intervention caused a strange consequence though, as he was changed into a woman.

During his nine years as a female, he married and bore children. He also became a priestess of Hera. When he came across another instance of two snakes mating, he again struck them with a stick and returned to his original male form.

In what can only be called an Olympian parlor bet, Zeus and Hera confronted Tiresias, asking him for whom sex was more pleasurable, men or women. The two gods believed that it was the sex opposite of theirs who enjoyed the greater ecstasy. Tiresias answered that sexual intercourse was more pleasurable for women. Enraged at the answer, Tiresias was struck blind by Hera.

Zeus could not restore Tiresias's sight; however, he did give him the gift of prophetic sight.

Hermes was the messenger of the gods. He was the son of Zeus and Maia. Among his other attributions, he was also the god of thieves, trade, athletes. He also guided souls to the underworld.

Hermes was a notorious trickster. While still an infant, he leapt from his cradle and hid Apollo's cattle. Apollo realized what was happening and confronted the child. Hermes insisted that he had nothing to do with it, so Apollo brought him before Zeus in a rage. Zeus, however, thought the matter was hilarious.

Like many of the other Olympians, Hermes was quite the philanderer. He never married, but fathered many children with over forty different women and goddesses.

He was also a patron to inventors, and is said to have invented music, numbers, the alphabet, astronomy, measurement, and many other indispensable creations.

Hestia was the goddess of architecture, the hearth and home, domesticity and the family. She was a daughter of Cronus and Rhea. She was a passive goddess, and is not always considered to be one of the twelve. In other myths, Dionysus replaces her on Olympus.

She remained a virgin, despite the advances of Apollo and Poseidon. She was directed by Zeus to tend the

Olympian fires. With any sacrifice, as Hestia was the oldest child of Cronus and Rhea (and the last to be purged, therefore also the youngest), Hestia was the first goddess to receive an offering.

Persephone was the daughter of Demeter and Zeus, and consort of Hades. Thus she was the goddess of the underworld. She is identified with the growth and productivity of the seasons, due to the above mentioned abduction and residence with Hades during what are the winter months.

Every spring as she returned from the underworld, the plant life would spring back up. As she was symbolically reborn, so were crops and other plants which had lain dormant in during her time in the underworld.

Poseidon was the god of the seas, earthquakes, storms, etc. His weapon (and symbol) was the trident. Another bisexual god, Poseidon had many consorts and children. He was often referred to as the earth shaker, and was one of the Olympian gods who fought against the Titans.

He was in competition against Athena to be the patron god of Athens. Although he lost the contest, he would remain a chief deity among the Athenians.

In Homer's Odyssey, he was angry with Odysseus (or Ulysses in Latin) for blinding one of his children, a

Cyclops. The god of the sea was infuriated, and set about making Odysseus's journey as difficult as possible. He, in fact, tried to kill Odysseus on more than one occasion, but was always thwarted.

Although much has already been covered in regard to Zeus (and much more will be covered) it seems fitting to give some information about the god outside of his poisoning his father Cronus, and his various infidelities.

Although the primary focus thus far has been on Zeus's various indiscretions (an accounting of his romantic endeavors alone would fill a few volumes), Zeus also had a protective side, especially toward Hera.

Ixion, king of the Lapiths in Thessaly, would come across Zeus in a way which was new to mortals of the time. According to myth, Ixion had married the daughter of Eioneus, but didn't pay the dowry. Eioneus, in order to have some assurance that Ixion would come to pay him, held his son-in-law's horses as collateral to ensure that payment would be made.

Ixion, however, was not about to give his new father-in-law his just dues. He lured Eioneus to his home, saying that he was ready to pay up, but killed Eioneus by casting into a flaming pit.

Killing a member of one's own family, in the myth, was unheard of, and those who could purify him refused to do so. Zeus, taking pity on the mortal invited Ixion to his table at Olympus, but Ixion's treachery was not over.

Ixion became enamored with, and began to pursue Hera. When Hera told Zeus about this, the king of the gods could hardly believe that one, especially someone in Ixion's position, would be so impudent as to make a move on his wife.

Zeus, as a test, created a cloud in the form of Hera (who would come to be called Nephele) and placed it in Ixion's bed (other stories have the cloud-Hera being placed in Hera's bed). Ixion had imbibed a few drinks at this point, and when he came across Nephele, he set himself upon it.

Zeus came in and, unable to deny Ixion's motives any longer, cast Ixion from Olympus, striking him with a thunderbolt. Ixion was bound to a flaming wheel, which was set to spin for eternity.

According to the myth, Nephele (cloud-Hera) had become pregnant through the dalliance with Ixion and gave birth to Centauros. Centauros would go on to mate with the horses of Mount Pelion, thus creating the race of Centaurs.

These are but a few stories related to the gods. The myths surrounding most of them are quite vast, and their essences are still about us today in popular and underground culture.

CHAPTER 4

Heracles and the Twelve Labors

Zeus (as is well established by now) was quite the playboy. How he ever got anything done between his affairs is astounding. However, one of his many children would come to be known as the divine hero. Quite possibly the most famous of Zeus's mortal children would be the one known as Heracles.

Heracles (the original figure from whom Hercules was adapted) was the son of Zeus and Alcmene. Zeus disguised himself as Alcmene's husband, Amphitryon, returning from the war of the time. He lied with her and swiftly departed. Later on that same evening, the real Amphitryon returned home. His wife, already impregnated by Zeus with Heracles, became pregnant that same night with the child of Amphitryon.

The hatred of Hera toward Heracles is legendary. This began its manifestation during Alcmene's pregnancy. Hera convinced Zeus to declare that the next high king would be of the house (a descendant of) Perseus (the founder of Mycenae, and the hero who beheaded the gorgon Medusa). Unbeknownst to Zeus, another child of that house was nearing its birth.

To ensure that the product of Zeus's infidelity would not become high king as intended, Hera went to Ilithyia, the goddess of childbirth, and tied Ilithyia's clothing in knots, her legs crossed. As no mortal could be born with Ilithyia in such a position without the intervention of a god, Heracles and his unborn twin half-brother were stuck in the womb of Alcmene.

Hera, in order to ensure the succession of another high king, caused the child Eurystheus to be born prematurely. He was now the one destined to become the high king while Heracles and his brother remained unborn.

Hera never intended for Heracles to be born at all. It was when one of Alcmene's servants came to Ilithyia and lied to the goddess, saying that the twins had indeed been born. Ilithyia, overcome by surprise, reacted with such a startled gesticulation at the news that her bonds were broken, thus allowing the twins to be born.

Alcmene offered up the child Heracles in an attempt to escape the goddess's wrath, however, when he was brought before her by Athena, Hera didn't know the child's identity. She nursed him, but the child's incredible strength caused Hera pain while nursing.

She removed the suckling child from her breast (the milk coming out to form the Milky Way).

Though Hera cast the child aside, he had consumed some of the milk, and with that, he acquired his powers. He was brought back to the house of Alcmene, and would be raised by them. Still fearing Hera's wrath, the child (who had originally been named Alcides by his mortal parents) was renamed Heracles.

This was not to be the end of Hera's attempts on the boy, however. When he was less than one year old, Hera sent two snakes to kill the young Heracles. Although his brother cowered, Heracles took the beasts to be playthings. He strangled them and played with them in his crib.

Heracles would grow to adulthood and marry a woman named Megara. The two had children, and life was good until Hera decided to intervene yet again. Sources differ upon exactly when, but what is consistent is that Hera caused Heracles to go insane. He believed that he was being attacked by evil spirits. He fought back against these dark beings, the battle ending in their easy slaughter. The problem was, these were no demons. In his madness, he had killed his children (in some myths he also killed Megara, however others have her departing and marrying his charioteer and nephew Iolaus).

Just as he was about to kill his mortal pater Amphitryon, Athena, known for her protectiveness of heroes, cast a stone into Heracles's chest, causing him to lose consciousness.

Now guilty of a sin which would require absolution, Heracles went before the oracle of Delphi, not knowing that the oracle was under the influence of his evil step-mother (history has a lot of those) Hera. The oracle advised Heracles to go before the high king and serve him in whatever way he should require. If he did so, Heracles was promised immortality, and a seat at Olympus.

The high king Eurystheus, an ally of Hera, was all too eager to have such a mighty servant. Although Eurystheus originally said that the debt of Heracles would be considered cleansed after performing ten heroic tasks, his requirements of the budding hero would come to be known as the twelve labors of Heracles.

The first labor was to kill the Nemean Lion, a ferocious beast with nearly impenetrable skin. Not only this, he was given only thirty days to complete the task. Let's just say Heracles and Eurystheus had issues. Heracles gathered arrows in order to slay the lion but the arrows bounced harmlessly from the lion's tough hide. Stories differ on whether he was finally able to strangle the lion to death, or whether he shot an arrow through the lion's mouth. Regardless, Heracles had indeed passed his first test.

Heracles tried to skin the lion, but could not break through its thick skin. It was only when Athena guided him to use the lion's own claws, that he was able to achieve the task. Heracles skinned the lion, and fashioned a cloak of armor from its impenetrable hide.

The king, upon seeing Heracles returning and carrying the dead beast on the thirtieth day, was petrified. He forbade Heracles to enter the city again, and communicated the remainder of the tasks through use of a messenger.

The second labor of Heracles was to slay the Lernaean Hydra, a nine headed serpent. The hydra was spawned by Hera (surprise, surprise) in order to kill Heracles. Slaying the beast would prove to be an even more difficult trial than the Nemean lion.

The Bibliotheca (fallaciously attributed to Apollodorus) gives a detailed account of the bout. The hydra *began* with nine heads, poisonous breath and even its tracks could kill a man. Heracles covered his mouth and nose to protect himself from the miasma of poisonous gas.

Heracles quickly went to work, decapitating the heads of the hydra one-by-one. Much to his dismay, however, with every beheading, the hydra would sprout two to replace the stump. He called for his charioteer (some say nephew) Iolaus for help. A new approach was developed including both of the men. Heracles would sever each head, and Iolaus would quickly cauterize the stump before two new heads could be sprouted.

This method worked quite effectively, although Hera wasn't done yet. She sent forth a crab to distract Heracles so that the hydra would be able to defeat the hero. Heracles, undaunted, stomped the crab beneath his foot.

The final head of the hydra became immortal, however Heracles was able to sever it with the use of a golden sword which Athena had given to him. The beast was slain. Heracles, always an opportunist, dipped the tips of his arrows in the blood of the poisonous blood of the hydra.

Unfortunately for Heracles, upon completing his tenth task, Eurystheus declared the slaying of the hydra improperly completed as the hero had the help of his nephew and charioteer.

The third task of Heracles was to be different. Heracles had proven himself against the fiercest of Hera's creations, and so Eurystheus set the next task to be the capturing of the Ceryneian Hind, an animal sacred to Artemis, able to outrun an arrow.

Heracles awoke one morning to glimpse the light reflected from one of its antlers. He gave chase to the animal, but it was indefatigable. He would chase it for the space of one year.

He eventually caught it, but on his return was confronted by Artemis and her brother Apollo. Heracles quickly explained and apologized for the situation. Artemis agreed to forgive him, so long as he let it go upon proving the hind's capture. Heracles agreed and, upon reaching the gates of the city, insisted that Eurystheus come and behold the animal for himself.

When Eurystheus came outside the city gates, Heracles, true to his promise let the hind go. He taunted Eurystheus, saying that the king had been too sluggish, and that it was his fault that the hind had escaped. It's not like the two were friends, but Eurystheus became more determined than ever to foil the hero's quest to become immortal.

The fourth labor of Heracles was to capture the Erymanthian Boar. He consulted a centaur for guidance, and was told to lead the boar into thick snow. By these means, he was able to capture the animal. He returned to the centaur. The centaur was overcome with fear at the sight of it. He begged Heracles to dispose of the boar, and Heracles obliged.

As the fifth labor, Eurystheus decided to not only present Heracles with a near impossible task, but to humiliate him in the process. The fifth labor was to clean the stables of Augeas in one day. Augeas, no doubt excited to learn that his stables would finally be cleaned, offered Heracles one-tenth of his herd, should the hero be able to finish the job in the space of a day.

While certainly being demeaning work, Eurystheus felt that the labor would be futile, as the stable housed over a thousand immortal cattle which produced an epic amount of droppings. To add further difficulty, the stables had not been cleaned in over thirty years.

Heracles, always persistent, rerouted two rivers, the Peneus and the Alpheus to run through the stables, thus washing them clean. Augeas, thinking the task impossible in such a short time-frame, rescinded his offer to the hero, claiming that he had already been instructed to carry out the cleaning anyway. In many myths, upon completion of his labors, Heracles would return to kill the reneging stable-owner.

After his tenth labor was complete, Eurystheus would declare this task to be forfeit as the slaying of the hydra, due to the fact that it was not Heracles, but the rivers which cleaned the stables.

The sixth labor of Heracles was to kill or drive away the Stymphalian birds. These, true to form, were no ordinary birds, but creatures with bronze beaks, and metallic feathers which the birds could use as projectiles to fend off any possible predators. And, as if Heracles hadn't waded through enough feces, the droppings of the birds were poisonous.

Heracles went to the swamp where the birds dwelled, however, he was unable to make his way closer to them as he would sink in the soft ground. Athena came to the rescue once again, presenting Heracles with a rattle, made by Hephaestus. Upon shaking it, the birds were frightened and took wing. He killed many of them with his bow, while the rest would fly away.

The seventh labor was to capture, but not kill, the Cretan bull. This bull had been causing all sorts of havoc in Crete. The king of the time (mythical King Minos) was quick to offer his aid, but Heracles refused. He was able to come up behind the bull and beat it to within an inch of its life.

He had the bruised and beaten bull sent back to Eurystheus who intended to sacrifice it to Hera. The goddess, however, refused the sacrifice, and Eurystheus let the beast go.

The eighth labor was to capture Diomedes's horses. The task may have seemed simple at first, but Heracles soon came to the knowledge that the mares were wild, likely caused by a steady diet of human flesh.

Diomedes was hardly keen to have his horses taken. In a common version of the myth, Heracles refused to sleep during the night, fearing that Diomedes would try to kill him in his sleep. He snuck in and severed the chains which held the horses.

He then spooked them to the top of a peninsula, took his axe and cut the land around the peninsula and thus trapped the horses on his self-made island. Heracles killed Diomedes and fed him to his horses which calmed the man-eaters down enough for the hero to bind their mouths and return them to Eurystheus.

The ninth labor was a task for the petulant king's petulant daughter. She coveted the girdle of Hyppolyta, the queen of the Amazons, and so her father Eurystheus commanded the retrieval of the belt to be the ninth labor.

Heracles set sail with some of his companions and, upon landing on the shores of the Amazon's territory, told the Amazonian queen of his task. The queen was impressed, and offered to give the girdle to Heracles without protest, even though it had been a gift to her by the god of war Ares.

Hera, however, just couldn't stay out of things, and disguised herself, slandering Heracles to the Amazons. She told them that his real purpose was to kidnap their queen and the Amazons quickly attacked him and his ship.

Heracles fought off the Amazons, killing their queen and taking the girdle from around her. He set sail, and delivered the belt to Eurystheus.

The tenth labor (which was supposed to be his last) was for Heracles to return with the cattle of the monster Geryon. This task was in a far off land, and so Heracles had to do some traveling.

He reached the desert of Libya and, while trudging through it, became angry at the excessive heat. To vent his displeasure, he shot an arrow at Helios, the Titan who carried the sun through the sky. While the arrow missed its target, Helios was so impressed by the feat that he offered his golden cup to assist Heracles in his travels through the desert. This cup was the means of by which Helios made his conveyance from the west (at the end of the day) to the east (to begin the next day). By using this cup, Heracles was able to reach the land of Erytheia where Geyron and his cattle lived.

Upon disembarking, Heracles encountered a two-headed dog named Orthrus. He made short work of the animal, killing it with his club. The herdsman in charge of the cattle tried to join Orthrus in fending off the hero, but was himself slain.

Alerted by the sounds of fighting, Geryon sprang into action. The monster, depending on the source, either had three heads and one body, or one head and three bodies, either two or six legs; various combinations of Geryon's anatomy are recorded.

The monster donned his armor and set off to attack Heracles. The hero, however, shot Geryon with one of his hydra-poisoned arrows with a force that sent the arrow through the monster's forehead, killing him.

Now at his leisure, Heracles collected the cattle and traveled back to Eurystheus. In one version of the story, the cattle are stolen by a giant named Cacus while Heracles is sleeping. The giant dragged the cattle backward so as to confuse the hero, should he go looking for them.

Heracles would find the trail, finding a cave with an enormous stone set in front of it (by Cacus). Heracles, quite the strong figure himself simply tore the top from the mountain and did battle with the giant. He slayed his foe, but Hera turned herself into a gadfly and proceeded to bite the cattle, causing them to scatter. Over the space of a year, Heracles would find all of the cattle, and so he made his way back to Eurystheus, thinking it to be for the last time.

Eurystheus, however, rejected two of the labors (the killing of the hydra and the cleaning of the stables), and insisted that Heracles was not yet finished. He therefore set two more tasks ahead of the hero.

The eleventh labor of Heracles was to gather the golden apples from the garden of Hesperides. The Hesperides were nymphs who tended the garden where the golden apples grew. According to one myth, these golden apples would grant the one who ate of them immortality for the space of one day. An individual could, in theory, eat an apple a day and become immortal. (There's a rhyme in that some-where).

Upon reaching the garden, Heracles came across An-teus, a being who was immortal unless he was sepa-rated from his mother Gaia. Heracles, upon discover-ing this, lifted his foe from the ground and crushed him in his strong arms.

Heracles reached the garden, but was unable to re-trieve the apples on his own. He went to Atlas, the Titan holding up the sky, and made a deal with him. Heracles would hold up the sky and Atlas would re-ceive a rest from his duties for the time it took the Titan to retrieve the apples (I think we see where this is going). Atlas quickly agreed and Heracles took to holding Uranus from Gaia.

Upon Atlas's return, however, the Titan refused to return to his post. Heracles, not willing to give up his quest and acquiesce to being the new form of separation between the sky and the earth, tricked Atlas into resuming his duty by asking the Titan if he would hold the sky long enough for Heracles to adjust his cloak. Atlas agreed (and I think we see where this one's going too) and Heracles quickly made off with the apples.

The hero returned, giving Eurystheus the golden apples, ready for his twelfth and final labor.

The twelfth labor of Heracles was to capture, but not kill Cerberus, the three-headed dog which guarded the underworld. Heracles was also not allowed to use any weapons in the tri-headed dog's capture.

The hero set out. He went to Eleusis in order to gain the knowledge of how to enter and exit the underworld while retaining his life. With the help of Hermes and Athena, he was able to enter the gates of the underworld at Tanaerum. He traversed the river Styx and, upon arriving in the underworld, opened up a dialog with Hades.

Hades agreed to allow Heracles to take Cerberus so long as he could capture the dog(s) without hurting him, and return the guardian dog(s) safely after the labor was complete. Heracles agreed.

Either before or after his conversation with Hades, Heracles came upon two men who were bound to chairs in the underworld. The men were Pirithious and Thesius, two men who had endeavored to kidnap Persephone so that Pirithious could take her as his wife.

Heracles was able to wrest Thesius from his chair, leaving a portion of the latter's thigh. Heracles was unsuccessful freeing Pirithious, however. It was said that the attempt shook the earth.

Heracles would finally come upon Cerberus. He was able to capture the Cerberus and didn't harm the dog in the process. He took Cerberus before Eurystheus, but when the king beheld the guardian of the underworld, he is said to have died of fright. (According to some myths, he simply cowered and told Heracles to return the dog to the underworld). Regardless what happened to Eurystheus, Heracles was now free of his debt for killing his children (and possibly wife).

The journey of Heracles was far from over, but he was finally free.

Martin R. Phillips

CHAPTER 5

Other Important Beings in Structure of Greek Mythology

The mythos of the Greeks was not limited to the major gods and the demigods (such as Heracles). A number of other characters would find an important role in the belief system of the ancient Greeks.

Prometheus was the most important character in regard to humankind, for he was their creator. The son of the Clymene and the Titan Iapetus, Prometheus did not participate in the direct conflict between the Titans and the Olympian gods (in other versions, he fought on the side of the Olympians). He was, therefore, spared their fate.

Prometheus fashioned the first human beings out of clay or mud and showed his creations to the goddess Athena. The goddess was so impressed that she breathed life into them. Thrilled by his creations being given life, Prometheus would teach the humans everything that he knew of math, science, and civilization. This would cause the first rift between Zeus and Prometheus.

Zeus, upset by Prometheus's indiscretion of teaching the humans the knowledge of the gods, made humankind mortal and cast them away from Mount Olympus.

At a dinner between gods and mortals, Prometheus presented Zeus with an option of two meals. One meal was that of an ox (unbeknownst to Zeus, Prometheus had set a meal of beef in the stomach of the ox), the other was that of gleaming fat (beneath which, Zeus would find only bare bones). Zeus, tantalized by the fatty plate, chose it as his meal. When he discovered that the plate was made up of bones which had been stripped of their meat, Zeus became furious with Prometheus.

Prometheus also gave humans fire. Accounts differ as to whether the humans already had the use of fire, but were stripped of it after Prometheus's fat and bones trick on the king of gods, or whether they didn't have fire in the first place. What is common though, is that Zeus at one point forbade the humans to be allowed the use of fire.

Seeing his creations suffering, Prometheus stole away the fire of the gods which Zeus had hidden and presented it to the humans, giving them (or returning to them) the use of flame.

For this, Zeus would levy one of his most extreme punishments. He had Prometheus chained to a rock where every day an eagle (a symbol of Zeus) would devour his liver. At night, the liver of Prometheus would regrow, allowing this cycle to continue on eternally.

Depending on the version of the myth, Prometheus was never freed from his bondage or, in some versions, was unchained by Heracles.

Perseus and Medusa

Medusa is, no doubt, one of the most familiar figures from Greek mythology. What is often not known about her is that she was once a stunningly beautiful, virginal priestess of Athena, the goddess of war and wisdom.

As Athena was a virgin, so too were all of her priestesses. Medusa had many suitors, but always held firm to her oaths of chastity. It was not only mortal men, however, that found Medusa irresistible.

The god Poseidon came to Medusa while she was inside Athena's temple on the hill of the acropolis. He viciously attacked and raped her. The act was not only a heinous violation of the young priestess, but a sacrilege to Athena.

Athena, however, did not take the side of her priestess. For the crime of *being* raped, Athena placed a terrible curse upon Medusa. Her skin was cracked and aged, her beauty turned to hideousness, her long hair was transformed into snakes and all who looked upon her would be turned to stone. Medusa was transformed into a gorgon.

Medusa was cast into exile, but quickly became hunted. According to the myth, even after Medusa was slain, her head would still cause any who looked upon her to turn to stone. Warriors came from all around to capture this tactical prize, only to be turned to stone in Medusa's growing rock garden.

Medusa would meet her match, however, at the hands of a warrior named Perseus. Danaë, the mother of Perseus, had been locked into a stone tower by her father Acrisius, the king of Argos. With no male heir, Acrisius consulted an oracle to discover whether his daughter would bear a grandson. The oracle instructed Acrisius that if Danaë were to become pregnant, her son would one day kill him and take his throne.

The theme of the older generation fearing their overthrow by a younger generation has persisted throughout the world, not only in myth and culture, but in real life as well.

Acrisius, fearing his as yet unconceived grandson, locked Danaë into the stone tower, expecting her to die from starvation as she was given very little food. The one thing that Acrisius hadn't prepared for, however, was the attention of the gods.

Zeus, always the philanderer, came through the window as a shower of gold. He impregnated Danaë with a son. When the news of his daughter's death never came, Acrisius went to investigate, finding his daughter holding her newly born child Perseus.

Afraid of offending Zeus, he didn't dare kill the two outright; however, he placed Danaë into a boat and set her adrift in the sea. They would eventually land on the island of Serifos. As Perseus grew, the king of Serifos became enamored with his mother. Hating Perseus, the king demanded that all occupants of Serifos provide him with a lavish gift; those who did not would be banished.

As Perseus was poor, the king expected him to be unable to present a fitting gift. In order to prevent the king from taking his mother as his wife and banishing him, Perseus promised the king that he would bring as his offering the head of Medusa.

The problem for Perseus was that he not only lacked any weapons, armor or knowledge of what Medusa looked like (as any who had actually seen her form would have been turned to stone), he also had no idea where he was going.

He prayed to the gods and, having heard his prayer, Zeus sent forth Hermes who gave the young man a pair of winged sandals. Hermes then told Perseus of a group of nymphs who would help him further. In order to find the nymphs, Perseus had to confront the Graeae, sisters of the gorgons.

The Graeae were three beings who shared use of one eyeball. In order to gain their cooperation, Perseus snatched the eyeball from the sisters and demanded that they tell him how to reach the grove of the nymphs. This was the same garden which Heracles encountered while searching for the golden apples.

Upon reaching the grove, the nymphs gave him a satchel within which Perseus could store the severed head of Medusa without fear of being turned to stone. Before he reached Medusa though, he would require much more.

He gained the necessary items by the kindness of the gods. Hades provided Perseus with a helm of darkness; Zeus gave Perseus an adamantine sword; and Athena gave Perseus the polished shield which would become iconic of the hero.

Now very well prepared for the confrontation, Perseus traveled to the island where Medusa had been exiled. By walking backward, he was able to view Medusa by looking at her reflection through the polished shield that Athena gave to him. By this means, he was able to sneak up on her and cut off her head.

When Perseus returned to the island of Serifos, he found his mother about to be married to the king against her will. The king had been making violent advances toward Danaë, and so Perseus, always protective of his mother used Medusa's head on the foul king. Acrisius had also come to attend the wedding and, justly enough, he too caught a glimpse of the gorgon's head.

Perseus would eventually offer Medusa's head to Athena as a tribute.

The Minotaur

Son of a human mother and a bull father, the Minotaur was one of the most feared of all the monsters in ancient Greece. Residing in a labyrinth on the island of Crete, the Minotaur lied in wait for a prisoner to enter its dwelling. Once found, the victim would be torn limb from limb and devoured by the ravenous beast.

The Minotaur was brought into being by an offense toward the god Poseidon by the king of Crete, Minos. The king had prayed to Poseidon to send a white bull, showing him favor and as the rightful heir to the throne of Crete. Upon its arrival, Minos had promised to sacrifice the bull to Poseidon; however, having become an admirer of the beauty of the bull, Minos reneged. (In another version of this story, Minos would slaughter the most prized new calf every year to Poseidon, but when the white bull was born, he couldn't bring himself to sacrifice it. Instead he slaughtered another bull, thinking that the god would call it even).

What is consistent in the myths is Poseidon's reaction to the sleight. He caused Minos's wife, Queen Pasiphaë to fall in love with the bull. The queen longed to copulate with the beast. She commissioned a great inventor named Daedalus to build her a wooden cow, hollow on the inside.

The queen took the decoy into the pasture where the bull lived, climbed inside and the rest is best left to the imagination. She became pregnant and, upon her delivery, the Minotaur (or bull of Minos) was born.

In an effort to turn lemons into lemonade, Minos decided to use the Minotaur to his own advantage. He commissioned Daedalus to envision and build a prison wherein the Minotaur would be placed, and any prisoners would be forced to face it.

Androgeus the son of Minos was in Athens, competing in Panathenaic Games, an early predecessor to the Olympics. He won every event, angering the other competitors. These men killed him. When Minos heard of this, he declared war on Athens.

In lieu of a full on attack, Minos demanded that seven male virgins and seven female virgins be offered to him as tribute to be sacrificed to the Minotaur once every nine years. This repeated until the third cycle when Theseus, son of not only the king and queen of Athens, but of Poseidon as well.

Having this dual paternity allowed Theseus to be an heir to the Athenian throne and also possess some of the powers of the gods. When he grew, the third set of virgins was rounded up, and he joined with them, vowing to bring down the terrible beast which had killed those sent before him. Having grown enough to retrieve his father's sword from beneath a boulder (where Aegeus, the king of Athens and father of Theseus had placed it), Aegeus had only one request of his son. Should he survive and return home, he should raise the white sail instead of the black sail in order to show his father that he lived.

When Theseus arrived at Knossos, the capitol of Crete, he quickly caught the eye of Ariadne, the daughter of king Minos. She fell in love with him and went to Daedalus in order to find some way to help the young man return from his imprisonment in the labyrinth. Daedalus gave her a clue (or ball of string) so that she could offer Theseus a way back to the entrance of the maze. She had one condition though. If Theseus survived, he would have to agree to marry her. Theseus agreed.

The fourteen virgins were led the next morning to the entrance of the labyrinth and locked inside. With his ball of twine, Theseus would lead the way. He bore the sword of Aegeus, and made his way in the dark through the labyrinth, searching for the Minotaur.

By the time his clue was one-quarter the size it had been upon his entry, Theseus comes across the sleeping Minotaur. Theseus ambushes the bull-headed creature, catching him off guard. The two would do battle: the Minotaur wielding an axe, Theseus with a sword.

The two do battle, but Theseus quickly has the upper hand. He corners the Minotaur and is able to slay him, but he's not out of the woods yet. Day is approaching and, should Theseus and the other virgins be caught by king Minos, they will surely be slain. He quickly makes his way back through the labyrinth, following the string that Ariadne had given him. Theseus and the others would escape in the dark of the night. Before dawn arrived, Ariadne met Theseus on the Athenian's boat and the group set sail toward Athens.

Aegeus, Theseus's father, had gone to a cliff overlooking the sea every day in order to ascertain his son's fate. When the ship came into view, Theseus had neglected to raise the white sail. Aegeus, thinking his son to be dead was so distraught that he cast himself over the cliff and to his death. These waters would come to be called the Aegean Sea.

CHAPTER 6

Greek Mythology and Homer's Iliad and Odyssey

Before ending, the myths and legends described by Homer in Iliad and Odyssey bear some investigation.

The stories of Homer's Iliad and Odyssey were originally communicated through word of mouth by travelling bards. They were collected by Homer (and possibly altered to fit into Homer's own sense of the story). While a brief synopsis of each will be given here, I also encourage you to read these two epics. They have been an inspiration in culture and literature since their original telling, over 2,500 years ago.

Iliad

Homer's Iliad begins near the end of the Trojan War. The Achaeans (or Greeks) are battling the Trojans. A priest of Apollo offers Agamemnon, the king of the Achaeans, vast wealth in exchange for Agamemnon to return his daughter Chryseis. Agamemnon refuses.

The priest then prays to Apollo for help and guidance and the god, a patron of Troy, sends forth a plague into the Greek camp which claims many lives. This plague continues for the space of nine days, until Achilles, hero of the Greeks and leader of the legendary Myrmidons, demands that Agamemnon return the girl to her father and end the plague.

While Agamemnon agrees to return Chryseis, he takes Briseis, a captive of Achilles, as recompense. Achilles is enraged and from that point refuses to fight. He also orders his Myrmidons to stand down. They threaten to leave the battle and the beach near Troy altogether. Meanwhile, Odysseus returns Chryseis to her father, thus ending the plague on the Greeks.

Mutinous, Achilles bids his mother Thetis, a goddess of the sea, to beseech Zeus and ask him to fight on the side of the Trojans. He does this in order to either convince Agamemnon to appreciate how much he needs Achilles and his Myrmidons, or bring a swifter end to the war. Zeus agrees, and the tide is turned.

Agamemnon has a dream that night, sent by Zeus, instructing him to attack the city walls. Upon his awakening, Agamemnon decided to test the morale of his soldiers by telling them all to head home. With the recent plague and the refusal of Achilles and his Myrmidons to fight, the soldiers were very nearly routed. It was only by the intervention of Athena, through the mouth and actions of Odysseus that the Greeks remained. He challenged and killed a discontented soldier for airing his grievances about the continued combat.

Word of the Greeks' pending attack reaches Priam (king of Troy) who then sets his own men out to the battlefield. As the armies approached each other, Paris, the prince of Troy and man who had stolen Helen from the Greek Minelaus, the act which purportedly started the war, (see previous chapter's section regarding Paris and the three goddesses), offered to fight a duel with the vastly superior warrior Minelaus to decide the victor of the war. Paris was no match for Minelaus, but was spared by Aphrodite before he could be killed.

At the intervention of Zeus, an arrow takes flight and wounds Minelaus, thus breaking the temporary truce and rejoining the battle. One of the great warriors on the side of the Greeks is Diomedes. He kills many soldiers, including Pandaros, the man who released the arrow wounding Minelaus. Aphrodite intervenes, but is wounded by Diomedes. Apollo then comes forth and warns Diomedes against battling against the gods, but the latter is not dissuaded.

The gods of Olympus were split in regard to their support of the armies, and Diomedes wounds yet another deity, Ares, who shrieks out in a very un-war-god-like cry (see above section on Ares).

After rallying his forces, Hector (brother of Paris and prince of Troy) reenters the city to bid the people toward prayer and sacrifice. He returns to the battle and confronts Ajax, a mighty Greek warrior. The two fight to a stalemate as the sun goes down.

The next day, the two armies agree to a day's peace so that they can burn their dead. The Greeks also erect a wall for protection. Paris refuses to return Helen over the protestation of many of the Trojans. He offers instead to return a treasure he had stolen and much of his own riches, but this offer is in vain.

Upon the next morning, the gods are forbidden by Zeus to interfere in the battle. The Trojans are victorious on the day and drive the Greeks back to their encampment. The sun goes down and prevents the Trojans from assailing the walls, so instead, they camp on the field.

Meanwhile, Agamemnon is ready to do whatever necessary to convince Achilles to return to the battle. He sends two heralds along with the Greek warriors Odysseus, Phoenix and Ajax who also bear gifts to Achilles. The Myrmidon warrior refuses to return to battle unless the Trojans breach the Greek walls and attack their camps and ships with fire.

During the night, Diomedes and Odysseus kill a Trojan warrior and generally cause mayhem among the camps of the Trojan allies. When morning comes, Hector leads the charge against the Greeks. He is begged not to proceed by Polydamas, an oracle, but the prince continues onward.

Zeus, who had continued to prohibit the gods from interference, is lured to sleep by Hera so that Poseidon can intervene on the side of the Greeks. Upon waking, Zeus sends forth Apollo on the side of the Trojans to sway the tide of the battle back in the favor of the Trojans. Unfortunately for the Trojans, they reach the ships and cause Achilles to send his friend Patroclus into battle wearing his armor to rally the Greek soldiers.

The tide of the battle is again turned, and Patroclus kills one of the Trojan heroes, sending the Trojans into retreat. He pursues the Trojans back to the city walls and is confronted by Apollo himself. Patroclus is killed by Hector, thinking the warrior to be Achilles.

Hector takes the armor of Achilles as his own and chaos breaks out.

The news of his slain friend is enough to enrage Achilles. He swears vengeance on the prince of Troy and he stands at the gate of the Grecian walls and, inspired by Athena, thunders in rage at the Trojan army. The Trojans are terrified by the presence of Achilles and in the cacophony, the Greeks are able to retrieve the body of Patroclus, and they bring his remains back to their camp.

New armor is fashioned by Hephaestus, and Achilles dons the gifts, ready to avenge his friend by killing the Trojan prince Hector. The next morning comes, and Agamemnon again offers Achilles gifts, including the return of Briseis, but Achilles has only one thing on his mind: his revenge on Hector.

Though Achilles is aware that he is destined to die young, and is even warned by his horse of his own coming death, the warrior drives his chariot into battle. He slaughters the Trojans before him and, splitting off about half of the Trojan forces, proceeds to slaughter this entire group. He is confronted by the river god Skamandros, who is upset that Achilles had littered his waters with so many dead Trojans. The god is driven back, however and Achilles returns to battle.

The gods, having been released by Zeus from their bonds of non-interference, rejoin the battle. Achilles is tricked by the god Apollo and led away from the mass of the Trojan forces as they retreat into the city. Only Hector remains outside the city walls.

Despite his initial urge to stand and fight, as Achilles draws closer, Hector begins to run around the walls of Troy, trying to evade the hero. He runs until Athena intervenes, fooling the prince into facing Achilles. The battle doesn't last long.

Achilles ties Hector's body to the back of his chariot and drags the prince's corpse back to the Greek camp. Despite being visited in a dream by his friend Patroclus who urges Achilles to bury Hector and allow the usual honors to fall to the slain prince, Achilles continues to desecrate the body by riding it around the funeral pyre of Patroclus.

Having had enough of this, Zeus sends Hermes to bring Priam to the tent of Achilles. Though initially confused by the Trojan king's presence, Priam's pleas compel Achilles to release Hector's body to the king. It is with the funeral of Hector that Homer's Iliad comes to an end.

Odyssey

The chronology of Iliad and Odyssey skips a number of years and a few important events which bear a mention albeit brief here. The city of Troy would fall to the Greek soldiers after Odysseus hatched a cunning plan during the funeral games for Hector, son of Priam.

The idea was to build a great wooden horse and present it as if it were a gift to the Trojans, honoring the god Poseidon. The Trojans brought the horse through their gate and into the city. Now unhindered, the Greeks only needed to wait until nightfall to spring from inside the horse and overtake the city.

The plan worked nearly to perfection; however, Paris, the one who caused the war and who cowered before Minelaus, shot Achilles through the heel with a poisoned arrow, killing him. Alternatively, one version of the story has Paris stabbing Achilles in the back while the latter was being married to Polyxena, one of Priam's daughters. Either way, Paris's slaying of Achilles never bears him any honor, and Achilles goes to his grave having never been defeated in battle.

Homer's Odyssey begins ten years since the end of the Trojan War and Odysseus has yet to return to his native Ithaca where he is king. The Odyssey is told, quite often, through the use of flashbacks. When the text begins, he is actually near the end of his journey, but the text reveals the ins and outs of his travels and tribulations.

Back at home, his wife Penelope is constantly beset by one-hundred and eight different suitors. These men believe Odysseus to be dead, and are quick to pounce on the opportunity for free food, drink, and the chance to possibly become king of Ithaca.

Penelope, while she despises the suitors, is bound by convention to feed these vultures. She refuses to take one as her husband, but can't turn them away either.

Much of the first books which make up Homer's Odyssey involve Telemachus, the son of Odysseus and Penelope. Athena, Odysseus's greatest ally disguises herself and tells Telemachus to search for information about his father's fate. Athena also approaches Zeus around this time, conveniently when Poseidon is not around. She would further help the young man by securing a ship for him (disguised as Telemachus himself). She would also stand at his side while the young prince conferred with the townspeople about what should be done with the suitors.

Poseidon's hatred of Odysseus is one of the main themes, and certainly the main cause of the warrior and his men being so lost in their travels. The reasons behind this begin with Poseidon's siding with the Trojans in the war, and the false offering to the god in the form of the Trojan horse. However, this would only be the beginning of the sea god's hatred of Odysseus.

Telemachus would travel by ship to visit Nestor, one of the Greek warriors in the war against Troy, often considered to be the most respectable of the Greek warriors. He then travelled to Sparta and inquired of Minelaus and Helen (who had finally returned with her husband, thus rendering the Trojan War a needless conflict over a spousal affair). They told him that his father was most recently known to have been held captive on an island by the nymph Calypso.

Now the story shifts its focus to settle on Odysseus himself. Odysseus is indeed entangled by the nymph Calypso who, having fallen in love with him, keeps him stranded on her island for the space of seven years. It's only when Hermes, intervenes that Calypso finally releases Odysseus. She gives him supplies as Odysseus builds a raft for himself.

Poseidon, still angered with Odysseus, sinks Odysseus's craft. Luckily, Odysseus had his share of allies throughout his plight, and he is obscured by the sea nymph Ino. He swims to shore, but has not only lost his craft, but his clothing as well.

He wakes on the shore, roused by the sounds of women laughing with each other. He comes out of the forest and discovers the princess Nausicaa and her maids washing their clothes in the sea. The servants flee in fear, but Odysseus beseeches Nausicaa to help him. She takes Odysseus in, giving him clothing and shelter.

While a guest of Nausicaa and the house of Scherie (the island upon which he had landed), a bard recounts two tales, one of the quarrel of Achilles and Odysseus, and the other about an affair involving Ares and Aphrodite. Odysseus, who at this point hadn't shared his identity with his hosts, asked the bard to recount the first tale. He exposes his identity by not being able to contain his emotions at the bard's words. It is from this point that Odysseus recounts his travels after the end of the Trojan War.

He began his trip home with twelve ships, carrying all of his men. They raided the city of Ismaros in Cicones. While Odysseus insisted that they leave quickly after dividing up the women and plunder, the men refused. The Cicones attacked the next morning, killing many of Odysseus's men. He and his remaining forces were able to escape, but they had their casualties.

Odysseus and his men would then come across lotus-eaters, lazy people who did nothing but eat lotus. The lotus-eaters didn't harm Odysseus or his men, but gave some of them lotuses to eat. The men who ate them no longer wanted to return home, rather, they stayed behind to gorge themselves with lotus.

Odysseus and his remaining men were then imprisoned by the Cyclops Polyphemus. Odysseus was eventually able to free himself by blinding the Cyclops, but made the mistake of telling Polyphemus his name. The Cyclops then entreated his father Poseidon (of course it had to be Poseidon).

Now filled with renewed rage toward Odysseus and his men, Poseidon put a curse upon Odysseus that he should wander the seas for the space of a decade.

Odysseus briefly came upon a hint of good fortune when they stayed with the master of the winds, a being named Aeolus. The master gave Odysseus a bag which contained the north, south and east winds. The ships came just in sight of Ithaca and everything was going well until one night while Odysseus was asleep, his men greedily opened the bag, thinking it to be treasure, and released all of the winds contained within. The resulting storm would carry the ships backward, far away from Ithaca. They found Aeolus again, but he refused to help them further.

The men set onward again, finally coming to the island of the Laestrygonians, a cannibalistic tribe. Odysseus's ship was the only one who didn't enter the harbor, and was thus the only one spared from complete destruction.

He would later run across the witch and goddess Circe. Having been warned about Circe by Hermes, Odysseus took a drug called moly which prevented what was about to happen to half of his men from happening to him. As the men ate and drank, they were turned into pigs. When Odysseus was able to resist the magic, Circe agreed to return his men to their original form provided that Odysseus would love her. They stayed on this island for a year, until Circe finally gave Odysseus the knowledge of how to contact the dead for guidance.

Odysseus traveled to an island on the western edge of the world and came across many spirits, including a crewman named Elpenor who asked Odysseus to find and bury his body. Odysseus agreed and was then visited by a prophet named Tiresias. Tiresias instructed Odysseus on how to return home without losing all of his men (not eating the sun god's flocks), and informed him that he had angered Poseidon by blinding his myopic son. He also came across Achilles, Agamemnon, Heracles, Minos, Orion, and other characters. He is eventually beset by innumerable souls from the underworld asking of news of their relatives. He retreats and leaves the island.

He returned to the island of Circe, who instructed them on the final stages of their journey. They sailed past the island of the sirens, women whose voices so entranced sailors that they steered their ships into the rocks. All of the men with the exception of Odysseus plugged their ears with bee's wax.

Next they sailed between the whirlpool Charybdis and the six-headed monster Scylla. Many of his men were lost, but Odysseus and his remaining companions made it through to safety. They would land on the island where the sun god's cattle resided. While Odysseus was asleep, all of his men chased down, slaughtered and ate the cattle. Upon their departure, the ships were wrecked, and all but Odysseus (the only one who hadn't partaken in the offense toward Helios) were killed.

He would come ashore the island of Calypso. The nymph fell quickly and deeply in love with Odysseus and forced him to remain with her until Zeus (via Hermes) demanded that he be released seven years after landing on the island; thus bringing the guests of Nausicaa up to speed.

The attendants of the party quickly agreed to help Odysseus get home. They set forth while Odysseus was sleeping and delivered him to a harbor in Ithaca where he goes on to find his own slave's quarters. Athena disguised Odysseus that he might view with anonymity the state of his house and kingdom. The slave, a swineherd named Eurnaeus, took him in and fed him.

After regaling the local farmers with a false tale about his disguised self, Odysseus comes across his own son Telemachus who had just returned from Sparta, narrowly evading an ambush by the suitors of Penelope. He discloses his identity to his son and the two set out to kill the suitors.

While in the house, being patched up, one of the maids washing his feet recognizes Odysseus's scar and runs off to tell the lady of the house. Athena intervenes, causing Penelope to be deaf to the woman's words.

Athena again intercedes by telling Penelope the following day to hold a competition where whosoever of the suitors could string Odysseus's bow and shoot an arrow through twelve axe heads could have her hand in marriage.

Odysseus joins the contest himself and is the only one capable of stringing the bow. He easily fires an arrow through the axe heads and along with his son, Athena, Eurnaeus and a cowherd he slaughters the suitors. They also hang a dozen maids who had slept with the suitors or deceived Penelope, along with a goatherd who had ridiculed Odysseus.

He finally reveals his identity to Penelope. She is at first skeptical, but when she tests him about what kind of bed they shared, he tells her accurately that it surrounds a living olive tree.

The next day, he meets with Laertes, his father, who only accepts that it's really Odysseus after the latter faithfully recounts the orchard which the former had gifted him. The story isn't quite over yet though, as the parents of the suitors set forth to take revenge on Odysseus. In her final intervention of the tale, Athena comes forth as Mentor (the disguise she had used while Telemachus was beseeching the people before his journey to Sparta) and causes them to forget their anger. Thus, the Odyssey is complete.

These large and profoundly beautiful volumes can be summed up, but hardly done justice outside of their own text. Their inclusion here is necessary, as is their inclusion in any text about Greek mythology, however, I again encourage you to read these phenomenal works for yourself.

CHAPTER 7

Meet Your Roman Doppelgangers

When Rome conquered Greece, rather than abolishing the Greek's religion, they, like many groups before and after including the Christians in Rome, ascribed the existing gods of the Greeks to aspects of their own mythology.

This was particularly easy for the Romans, as the Greek religion bore many similarities to their own, in fact, had likely inspired their own. The king of the gods in Greece, Zeus, would be attributed to the Romans' god Jupiter, a god of a similar nature. Ares would become Mars, Aphrodite would become Venus, Poseidon would become Neptune, Athena would become Minerva, and the list goes on.

The reason behind absorbing the religion of the Greeks rather than replacing it outright was simple. If conquerors take over your empire and strip you of your worship, they will be met with force and rebellion. In order to secure a more thorough and a much more peaceful transfer of power, the Romans would simply assimilate the gods and myths of the Greeks into their own system of belief.

This tactic has been used by conquerors and religious groups throughout the ages, notably by Christians. Once a powerful group, and no longer quite so persecuted in Rome, the Christians adopted the pagan holidays as their own. Although Christ is said to have been born in the summer or early fall, the Christians moved the date of his birth to be celebrated on December 25th, over the Roman pagan holiday of Saturnalia and also the birthdate of the Egyptian god Horus (among many others). Likewise, the festival of Easter which is celebrated as the resurrection of Christ is based off of the spring equinox and a pagan festival of fertility (and others). The festival celebrated Ishtar, a Babylonian goddess of fertility who was killed and resurrected.

By adapting the gods of the Greeks, the Romans ensured that the people would not rebel to nearly as great an extent over their rule. In fact, the Romans tended to respect the ancient Greeks and their manner of worship, and even added solely Greek legends and myths to their own pantheon.

This was quite out of character at the time for the Roman conquerors who often demanded more than simple fealty to the emperor. The Greeks were allowed to continue practicing their religion as they had done before this time.

CONCLUSION

It has been a long journey. From Chaos to Heracles, from the birth of the Olympian gods to the Roman adaptation of the Greek religion, the culture and mythology of the Greeks never ceases to fascinate people from all over the world.

We have read of heroes and heretics, gods and men. The tales of Greek mythology are vast and intricate, describing not only the forces of nature, but the innermost being of the Greek people, indeed, of all people in their own inventive way.

The Greek perception of death is visited by the dreaded gorgon Medusa. Life is brought forth by Prometheus. Not to mention all of the trials of Odysseus as he searches for his way home.

In learning about other cultures, we learn not only about our past, but our present as well. There is a common thread within all of us, and that can be found in the way that we relate to each other. The world is often beset by troubled times, but there is always the opportunity to come together through understanding and a commonality which runs deeper than any disagreement or perceived difference.

Whether you read this text casually or for the purpose of gaining specific knowledge of the ideas, philosophies, myths and manners of the Ancient Greeks, I certainly hope that you found in this book the object of your intention.

It has been a great pleasure to share this wonderful collection of Greek myths with you, the reader, and I hope that you will join in further reading of the other books in this series. The other books in this series include a book regarding the history of ancient Greece, along with one book each of ancient Egypt's history and mythology. I hope to meet you again through the age-old sharing of ideas that is the connection between myth and history, science and religion.

PART 2
EGYPTIAN
MYTHOLOGY

Ancient Secrets of the Egyptians

INTRODUCTION

The mythology of ancient Egypt is a vast and fascinating thing to study. With up to seven-hundred gods and goddesses (and combinations thereof,) the mythology of the ancient Egyptians was complex and, like all religions thus far, would undergo changes in theory and practice over time.

There's something so compelling about the ancient Egyptians that their culture and beliefs are still popular today. Although most of the country no longer practices the religion of the ancients, figures such as Isis, Osiris, Horus and Set (to name a very few) still pop up in movies, music, art and philosophical discussion.

The mythology of the ancient Egyptians is now worldwide, and is without doubt, one of the most enduring and fascinating sets of mythos that the world has ever seen.

One of the most intriguing things about the Egyptian mythology is that there are actually a number of parallels between it and later mythologies, such as that of the Greeks, the Romans; even modern day Judaism, Christianity and Islam have many similarities with these ancient myths.

But there is that which sets the mythology of the ancient Egyptians apart. Somehow it's regal and elegant. Like many other mythologies, there are tales of good and evil, sex and violence, creation and destruction, love and loss. The phenomena of nature, humans, animals, emotions, life, love and death are contained within the vast and often inscrutable sources from which we have come to glean the meaning behind the glyphs and learn more about one of, if not the most, important cultures and mythologies the world has seen.

It's important to note that many of the Egyptian myths that we are aware of only began to be recorded during the old kingdom (approx. 2686-2181 B.C.) through use of what we now call The Pyramid Texts. These were prayers, myths and incantations carved into the walls of the burial chambers of ancient Egypt's most important figures to ensure their safe passage to the afterlife.

The origins of Egyptian mythology are lost to antiquity; however, what we do know is more than enough to keep one busy studying for a lifetime. The pharaohs would come to be regarded as gods upon the earth, incontestable gateways between all of mankind and the realm of the gods; however, little mention of the pharaohs themselves will be made in this particular text. Here, we are primarily concerned with that which is outside the realm of governance; at least as far as it doesn't concern the religion of the ancient Egyptians.

In Egyptian mythology, we have the idea of the soul, of justice, balance, both on earth in life and after death in an afterlife... for a very short period, we even see a transition from paganism (belief in multiple gods) to monotheism (belief in one god,) although this change would not last.

The principles and morals of the ancient Egyptians are brought to life through their mythology. One of the easiest ways of understanding a people is to familiarize one's self with their beliefs, whether religious or secular, and I am very excited to take this journey with you into a realm of better understanding one of the most enigmatic societies that the world has ever known.

CHAPTER 8

The Creation

There are many creation myths in the ancient Egyptian religion, and some were favored more than others by different cities within the upper and lower kingdoms. Just as Egyptians had many cults proclaiming one god to be of primary importance, or simply as patron to a particular group, these myths vary depending on locale and time period. Therefore, as a general rule—both in regard to the creation myths and the other myths contained within this book—one of the more popular versions of the myth will be written here, although I will make an effort, where possible and pertinent, to show some of where the myths differ.

For most parts of this chapter, the Heliopolitan (that is to say, originating in the city of Heliopolis) tradition will be used, as it was, at one point, the center of religious worship and spiritual illuminism for a time. In this tradition, we have the Ennead, or the nine original gods from whom all else was brought into existence. This will, however, be contrasted with the tradition of Hermopolis (City of Hermes, obviously a name later given to the city by the Greeks,) to give an account of the Ogdoad, or a set of eight original gods and the birth of Re (often Ra,) the sun-god.

In the beginning, according to Egyptian mythology, the universe was without form and void; all that existed was the chaotic, primordial waters of Nu (the abyss; alternately Nun.) From this abyss sprang forth Atum (or Tum, Tem, Re-Atum, Atum-Ra, etc.) Different traditions have the first god to spring forth from Nu to be different forms of the god Re, as Atum is particularly associated with the sun, or Re, at sunset, thus he is a god of completion. In the case of the previous philosophy, being the god of completion could reference the completion of the first formative god. Other Egyptian traditions also have Ptah, Amun or the entire Ogdoad as the original creators.

This relates to the later ideas of the ancient Greek religion, also Judaism, Christianity and Islam in that, though naught else existed, the world was formed over the course of days from a watery abyss. This is, of course, merely an extension and not verbatim the Egyptian myth, as the Egyptian creation story has Re, the sun, being the creator itself.

This god came into existence through formulation of thought and strength of his/her will. The reason why both feminine and masculine pronouns are covered here is that, like many ancient and modern gods,

Atum was hermaphroditic (that is, both male and female, thus able to create without unifying with another.) In other traditions, Atum was neither male nor female, although this may simply be a reference to his hermaphroditism. Regardless, in Atum was every element and particle necessary for all of creation to exist.

Traditions differ on when the next part happened in the sequence of things, but there is consensus that Atum called forth a pyramidal island called Benben. Thus, he had a place to steady himself, and some traditions have Benben eventually becoming the home of Atum.

Atum is notable, not only for being the progenitor of all of the gods after himself and Nu, but for his single, all-seeing eye. This eye will become of particular importance shortly.

Things really started to get going when Atum spat. This normally rude gesture produced two children: Shu (God of the Air) and Tefnut (Goddess of mist or moisture.) As with many mythologies, the gods of the ancient Egyptians, specifically the primordial ones (primordial meaning something which has existed since the beginning of time,) represent specific elements, forces or parts of nature. Thus Shu=Air and Tefnut=moisture, the basic components of the act of spitting, and also translatable into elements within the daily lives of the people.

At this point, however, the Earth itself had not been created. This didn't happen until Shu and Tefnut, through sexual union, parented Nut (Goddess of the Sky) and Geb (God of the Earth.)

After the birth of Nut and Geb, Shu and Tefnut decided to go for a leisurely stroll through the universe. This stroll was, in fact, so leisurely that their father, Atum became worried and sent his eye to search for them. It took quite the journey, but eventually came across the two wanderers who retrieved it and brought it back to their father. Upon witnessing their return (and, assumedly having his eye returned,) Atum wept. His tears would fall to the surface of the earth, and from these tears were formed human beings.

Things would get a little complicated when Nut and Geb came together and Nut was impregnated. Shu, somehow upset by the union of these siblings, his children, but completely fine with his relationship with Tefnut, his own sister, decided to separate the two by physically coming between them. In some traditions, Shu also prevented Nut from giving birth. Nut, understandably distressed by this development went to Tahuti (also called Thoth) and begged his aid. This led to a gambling match between Shu and Tahuti which the latter would win, thus allowing Nut to give birth. Who accepts a challenge from the god of wisdom (Tahuti) and thinks that they can win, anyway?

Nut (pronounced like newt or, in some traditions, Nuit, pronounced like "new eat") would, however, give birth to Osiris, Isis, Set and Nephthys. With that, the Ennead (the first nine gods) would be complete.

For a quick contrast in the interest of a broader perspective, in the Hermopolitan (originating from Hermopolis) creation story, things started with a group of eight gods called the Ogdoad. These gods were often broken up into either two sets of four or four sets of two. The reason for this being: Two sets of four = the male and female gods grouped together; four sets of two = the god and goddess representing each of the four primordial functions were grouped together (i.e. Nu and Naunet, etc.)

The gods were: Nu (male) and Naunet (female), representing the primordial waters; Kuk (male) and Kauket (female), representing the darkness of the waters; Huh (male) and Hauhet (female), representing the limitless expanse of the waters; and Amun (male) and Amaunet (female), representing the occult (meaning hidden) nature of the waters.

In this tradition, these gods all issued forth from the primordial waters themselves, and were depicted as creatures of the sea; specifically, the males were frogs and the females were snakes. This is the reason for the division of the eight into two sets of four. It was when these original gods came together that the mound Benben came out of the water, and another god shot into the sky. The god was Re. With that, there was light.

Regardless of which Egyptian creation myth you go with (and there are plenty of others from which to choose,) the most consistent similarities seem to be the origin of everything within the original and primordial chaotic waters, and the coming forth of Benben, the mound of earth which sprang from these waters.

At the time of creation, all was still in chaos, however. Though the world had been formed, and the sky and most of the rest of existence, including that of humans, there was no order, no law or justice. From this need, Ma'at (or Maat, Mayet, Maae't, etc.) was created. Ma'at was formed to bring the principles of honor, law and order to the still young universe, and it is according to this law that humans were expected to act, not only within the myth itself, but in daily life. Ma'at would also go on to play a very important role within the Egyptian conception of death and the passage to the afterlife, but we'll get into that a little bit later on. Ma'at's symbol is that of the feather, specifically that of an ostrich.

Ma'at was the daughter of Atum (or Re, depending on which personification of the sun-god is used in the particular creation myth.) Not only would Ma'at bring the world and, indeed the universe itself, out of the realm of chaos, through her influence, it would not be able to return into chaos. The exact time within the creation myth of Ma'at's creation is debatable. Some myths have Ma'at being born at the beginning of the universe and thus, the universe was able to be brought from pure chaos; in others, she was born shortly thereafter. Regardless, she is not considered to be the original progenitor of the universe, rather a function of it.

Though many of the gods of Ancient Egypt were favored, disfavored, some even ignored or not believed in, Ma'at was a constant throughout the cities of Egypt for her importance as a living principle to the people throughout the kingdom.

Martin R. Phillips

CHAPTER 9

How to Usurp a God

With so many different Egyptian myths, it's difficult to know where to start after the creation, however, Isis and Osiris, Set and Horus play an integral role in the way that things would play out shortly after the world was born. Horus, specifically, would become an extremely important figure within the Egyptian pantheon; although Osiris and his wife—and sister (this happens a lot in mythology)—were also of the utmost importance. The myth of Osiris is quite probably the most intricate of all of the Egyptian myths, as it would set the stage for the way the world would work from his rule onward. As usual, there are different versions of the myth, but we'll focus on the most commonly known one, with occasional interjections with some of the differences.

When the world was formed, Osiris (god of life, rebirth, and [spoiler alert] the afterlife) was king of the Earth. Isis was his queen. Though not much is known (or possibly, was formulated) about the time in which Osiris ruled, other than that he was a just ruler and followed the order of Ma'at, the consequences of his brother Set's anger toward him, is where the importance of the story really came to the forefront.

According to the myths, things were going fine, right up until Set (god of disorder, the desert, storms and often thought of as the Egyptian equivalent of the devil, or the Hebrew Shaitan—meaning adversary— later translated into Satan) murdered Osiris. Exactly why he did this, as I'm sure you've already become accustomed, changes depending on where the story was told, but the predominant myths have Set as being jealous of his brothers rule, and his murder was intended to usurp him; Set killing Osiris due to a kick or other blow that Osiris had given him; or Osiris copulating with Set's wife (or consort as historians generally put it,) Nephthys. Regardless the reason, Set killed Osiris.

In Egypt, it was believed that what was written had power to affect reality. Due to that, there is not too much extant regarding the murder itself, although some versions of the murder do exist, one of which has Osiris drowned in the Nile. This version, however, does not coincide in most ways with the general myth of Osiris and was written by a Greek, for Greeks after the ancient Egyptian civilization as an independent, autonomous state had come to an end. Its inclusion here is simply for lack of a more accurate myth of the actual death of Osiris.

In this version of the myth, written by Plutarch (46-120 AD; Greek historian,) Set tricks Osiris into his death. This process started by gathering seventy-three conspirators, one of whom was no lesser person than the Queen of Ethiopia. Set then fashioned an incredibly ornate, man-shaped box which would fit Osiris exactly. Then what does every good murder plot need? A dinner party.

At the party, the ornamental box was greatly admired, and Set announced that he who would fit perfectly inside the box would be named its owner. Many tried to make themselves fit within, but it was clearly not a fit. When Osiris stepped forward and into the box and (surprise, surprise) he fits perfectly. It's right about this time that the lid to what would be, according to Plutarch, the first sarcophagus would be slammed shut with Osiris inside and is sealed. Set and his conspirators dumps it into the river, thereby drowning him.

According to Plutarch, and possibly due to the already high level of reverence for the Nile itself because of its importance to the ancient Egyptians, people who died by means of drowning in the waters of the Nile were held in particular esteem, even sacred.

Although the story of Osiris doesn't end here in Plutarch's myth, there is enough from original Egyptian sources to pick up from this point and, as this isn't a book on the Greek interpretation of Egyptian mythology, therefore we'll go back to the more accurate-to-the-Egyptian telling.

Upon his death, the body of Osiris is dismembered, scattered and hidden (some earlier myths had Osiris simply killed and hidden away.) The number of pieces (or whether there was dismemberment or not) varies, but one of the most functional is that of forty-two, the number of nomes (Egyptian cities) in Egypt.

Isis (wife of Osiris and benefactress of fertility, motherhood and magical power,) upon hearing of her husband's death sets out to find his body. In some versions of the myth, she travels with Nephthys (goddess of the night, of death, lament and, interestingly enough, service,) Tahuti (god of wisdom, magic, writing {specifically hieroglyphic writing} and knowledge,) and Anubis (often wrongly attributed as the Egyptian god of death, Anubis is actually the god of embalming and other funeral rituals) during this search. It is from the joining of Anubis in the search and eventual finding of Osiris that the ritual preservation of bodies through embalming, mummification and the necessary processes contained therein were said to have originated.

Later myths equate the yearly flooding of the Nile with the tears of Isis for her slain husband, or other causes relating to the death and rebirth of Osiris.

Meanwhile, Set is sitting pretty on his throne of the Earth (or in some myths, there is simply a gap in kingship.) Before Osiris is made whole, Set and those who follow him attempt to further destroy the body of Osiris so that he cannot be made whole again. They are fended off by those who seek to restore Osiris to life.

When the body of Osiris is found, or collected (in some versions, all but the phallus are recovered, as it was cast into the Nile and eaten by a fish... lovely,) he is again made whole. He is resurrected and impregnates Isis with Horus. Their copulation is usually referenced either through a union while she is in the form of a bird {kite or hawk} and restoring him to life, or by a bolt of lightning. In another, Isis fashions a phallus for her dismembered (if you don't get the pun, I'm not going to explain it) husband, and it was through use of this that she became pregnant with Horus.

Not too much is known about the period of Osiris's revival before his descent into the Duat, or Egyptian underworld (over which he would become the ruler,) but this act of resurrection would set the tone for the entire realm of Egyptian mythology. Through the death of the god and his subsequent resurrection, it would become possible for all people to enjoy an afterlife through him, though they would have to pass the test of Ma'at (will be discussed in more detail in the following chapter) or righteous living in order to gain entrance to the afterlife. This ideal was not the first of its kind and far from the last.

The Osiris myth can technically be said to end with the conception of Horus, at least as an active process of Osiris outside of Duat, however, the storyline is just beginning.

Being all-too-aware of Set's murderous victory over Osiris, and knowing that Set probably wouldn't let a child of Osiris live too long, as he may pose a threat to the throne, she hid herself away in Akh-bity, a papyrus thicket in the Nile Delta of Lower Egypt. It would be here that she would give birth to Horus (Greek version of the name. The Egyptian name would be Hoor, Hor or Har, meaning, "The Distant One.") This part of the myth is quite similar to Greek mythology, when Rhea, the mother of Zeus would hide him away to protect him from his father Cronus.

During Horus's youth, he wasn't yet the powerful god of war that he would become. In fact, he was quite vulnerable. Different accounts say different things about whether the malady which befalls Horus simply happened or was orchestrated by Set, but the important takeaway is a look at how the Egyptians used the idea of the young god falling prey to illness or attack.

Many texts were written, considered to be magical in nature, which would heal a person of a particular malady by claiming that malady is what befell Horus. As an example, if a person came in with a stomachache, the text for healing would have Horus being affected in the same manner. Quite possibly the most common ailment is that of a snakebite. It is through Isis's own magical powers (alternately through the powers of Ra or Geb,) that Horus is healed, and thus that the person seeking the magical help which the texts would provide would be healed through the same process.

Horus would be healed, and grow to adulthood.

With Osiris resurrected and now god of the dead, Horus might have let bygones be bygones, but the fact remained that Set had killed his father. To put it colloquially, Horus was pissed.

In some traditions, Set and Horus were actually brothers who vied for the right to be named king of all. This version will be referenced, but not the main focus in this continuing section.

When he came of age, Horus would challenge Set. To the victor would go the spoils; in this case, the throne. The conflicts of Horus and Set for rule would come in many varieties, and would last for a space of eighty years.

Quite possibly the most extensive source for these battles is referred to as "The Contendings," wherein

Horus and Set compete in a number of different ways. The first was that they brought the argument over who should be king of Egypt before the Ennead after Horus challenges Set.

Although most of the gods of the Ennead believed Horus to be the rightful ruler, the judge presiding over the Ennead and their decision (Atem, Ra, or Geb, depending on the source,) thought Set should rule. Therefore, the two would compete with one another through various trials, competitions and even full-on battles with one another. They held a boat race which Horus won and many other such events in which Horus would always prevail, however, the judge was not yet convinced and the contest would go on for eighty years.

One of their battles involved the two of them transforming themselves into various creatures to do battle. During this battle, both would lose an important piece of themselves at the hands of the other. Set's testicles were lost (or in some cases, damaged.) This would signify a loss of creative energy and strength which would (arguably) prove to be Set's eventual downfall. Horus, on the other hand, lost one of his eyes.

The loss of one of Horus's eyes is of a particular kind of importance as, Horus being a solar god, it was believed that the sun was the right eye of Horus; the moon: his left. Thus it was his left eye which was plucked out, signifying the moon. It would eventually be returned to him, however, the loss of Horus's eye would explain the waxing and waning of the moon and the phenomenon of lunar eclipses.

In a particularly strange and somewhat disturbing episode, Set, known for his ravenous sexual appetite, made a deal with Horus. In this deal, Horus would allow Set to have sex with him, but in return, Set would give Horus a measure of his strength.

In one particularly important (and graphic) version, Set's intention was to show his dominance by implanting his seed within his long-time foe. Horus, through a manner which is best left to the imagination, caught the seed before it could enter his body.

The concept of "the male seed" (semen) was one of great power and purpose in the minds of the ancient Egyptians; and this can be referenced both by another version of this same story where Set's seed does enter Horus and makes him sick, and also by the continuation of the above version.

Sticking to the version where Horus catches the haughty god's... projectile... Isis and Horus decide to repay the intended offense by placing a measure of Horus's... dressing... onto a piece of lettuce which Set then consumed, not knowing what trick had actually been played.

The reason why this myth is so important in the story is that the two gods would then go before the Ennead again to be judged to find which of the two of them was dominant. It is around this time that the seed of Horus within Set becomes apparent through the "birth" of a disk upon his forehead. With this, Horus is finally named champion.

The championship of Horus over Set would play a particular importance to the Egyptians as their pharaohs believed themselves to be descendants of Horus, the rightful ruler of Egypt.

CHAPTER 10

Morality, Life, Death, and the Afterlife

Now, with some backstory, it is possible to better explain the concepts of the daily lives of the Egyptians. With Osiris now king of the underworld and his son, Horus, ruler of both lower and Upper Egypt, the stage is set for the more fundamental beliefs of the Egyptians.

First and foremost is that of Ma'at. Ma'at, as has been explained above, was the concept of order, truth, justice, honor and righteousness to the Egyptians. In order to fulfill one's requirements during their lives, one must live by the principles of ma'at. This meant balance, this meant fairness to one another, but always in fealty to the pharaoh, who was considered to be a god among men.

Ma'at was not only a concept to the Egyptians though, she was also a goddess who played an important role in the journey from this life to the next. Once the dead reached the Hall of Two Truths in the Duat, their heart would be weighed against the feather of Ma'at. If the heart weighed less than or equal to the feather, the person would continue onward and enjoy a pleasant afterlife; if, however, the heart outweighed that of the feather, it meant that the person did not lead a just life, and their heart was then fed to the goddess Ammit, and the person would then be forced to wander the Duat (the underworld) for eternity.

The above requires some explanation. The ancient Egyptians believed that the soul (or the ba) resided in the heart, and thus it was not merely the physical organ of pumping blood which was weighed, it was the person's very soul. When people died and were embalmed, all of their organs were removed except the heart, thus allowing them to opportunity to at least receive their judgment.

The Egyptians weren't known for leaving things to chance, however, and in burial tombs it is more than common to find a number of spells, carvings and/or incantations to offset the sins which they may had committed in their lives. This shows us two things: one, that the ancient Egyptians weren't above trying to bend the rules to get into the afterlife; and two, that they did not conceive of a perfect life as being possible, or at least very plausible. Everyone made mistakes, but it was possible, they believed, to alter their fates through these incantations.

There were many general principles that made up the conception of living a life of Ma'at, but there were certain types of crimes which could land a person in hot water. For instance, crimes against temples, priests or blasphemies against the gods were considered especially atrocious. Stealing from a temple, from the dead or desecrating holy spaces would fall under this.

Theft and murder were, of course, considered to be egregious offenses against Ma'at and one's fellow man, but so also were such things as ignoring the truth or being slanderous of a servant toward his or her master. Other crimes which could weigh heavily upon the heart included causing pain or hunger; harming animals for purposes not of self-defense or to satisfy hunger; withholding the rightful possessions of orphans, being aggressive and even eavesdropping or speaking without thinking first could also be weighed against a person. The goal was for a person to be able to say honestly, "I have done no injustice to people, nor have I mistreated any animal. I have done no wrong." (see Egyptian Book of the Dead, Chapter 125.)

Of course, in a system where losing one's temper was considered sinful (perhaps not a bad idea, methinks...) it was through the rites and the practices of the priests and the incantations and inscriptions left with the dead that many Egyptians believed they would be able to enjoy an afterlife, whole and in paradise.

As has been stated above, it is a common misconception that Anubis, the jackal-headed god was that of death, or of the afterlife; however, Anubis's part was in funerary rites, and the passage of souls. (The god of the dead and the afterlife was Osiris.) These rites included those of embalming, mummification, the incantations and various other processes meant to prepare the body and the soul for their journey through death and, hopefully, to the pleasures of the afterlife. It was Anubis who would weigh the heart of the deceased against the feather of Ma'at and determine the person's worthiness.

Ammit, the devourer of the hearts of the unjust, was either considered a goddess or a demon (more popularly, the latter) who had the head of an alligator, the torso of a lion and the hind-quarters of a hippopotamus. If Ammit devoured the heart, the person was said to not only wander between worlds, unable to continue on to be with Osiris, but that theirs would be a restless eternity, spent dwelling with only the memory of the mistakes they had made that had kept them from paradise.

It's no wonder that the peoples of ancient Egypt often sought the blessings and rituals of priests to ensure their passage through to the afterlife.

When the dead of those who had been successful enough in life to warrant such honors were put through their funerary preparations, a scroll would often be placed into their mouth to allow the deceased individual to regain his or her senses as they passed onward through the many stages on their ways to the Halls where their final judgment would be heard.

First, the deceased would travel upon the barque of the sun, the vessel with which Ra would recreate the world every day. This would be the symbolic and, in the minds of the Egyptians, the practical way that a person would be able to achieve rebirth and thus, eternal life. They would then pass to the land of wish fulfilment, also called the Field of Reeds, where they would be required to pass through seven gates on their way toward the halls of judgment. It was with the help of the spells provided for the deceased that they would then be able to pass along into the presence of Osiris.

It is in the presence of Osiris where Anubis would weigh the heart, and judgment would be made. The person would also be required to justify their life. Depending on the time period, Osiris had different levels of discretion over whether a person would be spared, but regardless, if the heart outweighed the feather of Ma'at, that was that.

Should a person pass the test, they would then be taken into paradise. If not, well, we've already covered that...

There are certain texts which relate stories regarding the true worth of a soul to the Egyptians, especially in regard to the impact (or lack thereof) of earthly success on one's chances to make it into the afterlife. Through the conception of the Egyptians, a person's material success, while pleasurable upon this plane, could actually be damaging in the next. This is in stark contrast to many cultures, but in complete agreement with the belief systems on which these same cultures are based today.

The worth (or weight) of a person's heart was measured in the emotions, the will, the intentions and the thoughts of the individual to which it had belonged. However, it is more than likely that the above mentioned dichotomy between what was believed and what was practiced was as schismatic then as it is today.

It's difficult to say exactly what the Egyptians were like on a day-to-day basis, especially those of the peasantry, the largest portion of the ancient Egyptian population (and, indeed, historically always the largest portion of any known society,) but it can be fairly assumed that the peasants were held to a higher standard. Although it's quite possible that many simply threw their hands in the air and conceded defeat as they wouldn't have been able to afford the more elaborate burial practices; it's also quite possible that many of them also sought to live according to Ma'at even moreso than their wealthier countrymen. Otherwise, how could they ever hope to even make it before Osiris?

Regardless one's ability to afford elaborate funerary services, one thing is certain: the idea of Ma'at and the pantheon of the Egyptian gods played a vital role in every part of ancient Egyptian society. Even the poorest members of the society had their funerary rites (so long as they weren't lost to the desert,) but these, of course would often differ in style or grandeur.

For instance, a wealthier individual (not to mention a pharaoh) would often be buried in a tomb with his or her possessions, including food, water, beer… you know, the essentials; but also sometimes with their servants, their spouses and even their pets. They would undergo the full embalming process and be adorned with numerous spells and incantations to grant them swift passage to and through the gates of the afterlife.

A poorer person, however, would much likelier have undergone a smaller ceremony with loved ones doing what they could to preserve their fallen, but often times, even though there were rites, these people would simply be buried in the desert.

As time passes, much is lost, but much is discovered. I'm sure that as people continue to investigate the practices of the Egyptians, we will learn more about their conceptions of morality, life, death and the afterlife of the Egyptians.

CHAPTER 11

The Pantheon and the Deeds of the Gods

Rather than just give you some boring list of the gods and their attributes, I find it much more engaging to pass along some of the stories of how the gods were perceived, and their purported actions. Over this chapter and, to a certain extent, the rest of the book, we will be taking a look at particular myths and how they may have impacted the lives of the ancient Egyptians. While much still has yet to be learned about the gods and goddesses of the ancient Egyptian religion, there is still much that we can glean, even from those we know less about than others.

Some of the gods have already been mentioned in detail, but are of such importance that they bear further investigation, but I will also endeavor to give as full a view as possible of the other gods (as space allows) their actions, and the myriad myths surrounding them. In a book like this, one can take any number of approaches, but I've found that what really sticks is the story.

One thing that is important to note is that in the Egyptian pantheon, gods oftentimes merged with one another as, to the Egyptians, there wasn't only one plane of reality or existence. These conjoined gods were often used in order to depict a specific principle that the two individually shared, and thus, by their combination, the association would become even stronger. A quick example of this is Amun-Ra, a combination of Amun and Ra. Therefore, at times, you will see one or more god's name in the same word, signifying this sort of union. Sometimes the myths overlap and seem to be quite contradictory to one another, but to the ancient Egyptian, these were all simply the complex dealings and natures of the gods themselves.

It is again important to note that at different times and different locales, different mythos surrounded the gods, nature and the Egyptian belief; therefore, I will simply be passing along some of the more popular myths. Let's begin with Hathor.

Hathor, in the earliest times of the Egyptian pantheon, was actually said to be the mother of Horus. This station would, of course, be taken by Isis for the longer period of the Egyptian religion, but Hathor was still of great importance to the Egyptians.

Hathor was the goddess of love and happiness, music and dance, and she was also the protector of women. Hathor is depicted as having the head of a horned cow, and was both wife and mother to the god Ra (also sometimes, his daughter.) It was believed that every morning, she birthed Ra, thus allowing the sun to rise; in this case, she would be the obvious mother. During the day, the two would copulate, and this is how she would become impregnated for the following day.

With the founding of the Middle Kingdom (2055-1560 B.C.) it was said that it was Hathor who made the victory of Mentuhotep II, then pharaoh of Upper Egypt, possible. This victory would unite Upper and Lower Egypt for the first time since the First Intermediate Period.

The way this was believed to have happened was that Ra, the sun-god and her consort (also in this case, represented by Mentuhotep II, or the pharaoh of Upper Egypt in general) informed Hathor that the people of Lower Egypt were planning to kill him. Hathor went into a rage and transformed herself into the goddess of war of upper Egypt, Sekhmet.

Historically, the war lasted nearly thirty years, but in this particular myth, it was Hathor in the personage of Sekhmet who laid the bloody destruction upon Lower Egypt. She had become literally bloodthirsty. When Ra beheld the extent of the carnage and the extent to which Hathor had lost control, he collected a large amount of the blood that she had spilled and mixed it with beer (yes, Egyptians loved their beer,) this he laid before her. Thinking the dark-red fluid was blood and only blood, Hathor/Sekhmet gorged herself upon it. She imbibed so much of the alcohol that she began to lose steam. Eventually, she became so drunk that she lost her bloodlust and was thus returned to her original form, thus ending the war and, somewhat unwittingly reunifying Upper and Lower Egypt under the rule of one pharaoh.

Next, we will take a look at Tahuti, also called Thoth. As god of wisdom and magick, he was often called upon to be an intermediary between the forces of good and evil. He was a scribe and was, in fact, said to have given hieroglyphics to the Egyptians. This Ibis-headed god was originally associated with the moon but, like most of the other gods in the Egyptian pantheon; he would gain a number of other associations such as those mentioned above.

Thoth is of the utmost importance throughout the mythology of Egypt as he was often the only one left who kept the balance between the forces of order and chaos. He was the husband of Ma'at, and the two stood on either side of the boat of Ra, which carried the sun through its course. He was self-begotten and, the Egyptians believed, not only extrapolated the necessities regarding the construction of all heavenly bodies and, indeed, all of existence, he also directed their motion.

In battles between gods, such as that of Ra and Apep, he would ensure that the natural order of things was maintained and that balance was kept. If one foe gained the upper hand by injuring his opponent, Thoth would heal him, so that things would remain in their balance, although the sun-god was always allowed to complete his travels.

The concept of Thoth in regard to the Egyptian mind and, indeed, that of the modern world is that of the necessity of good and evil, as one could not exist without the other. Thoth can be seen as the ultimate intellect; the one that not only understands all things, whether apparent or hidden, but actually causes change within them. For this reason, he is still studied and conceptually admired by many modern-day philosophers and others who seek to create change in their environment in accordance with their design. As the god of magic (sometimes spelled magick,) his name adorns books and tarot cards relating to some of the hidden knowledge with which it is believed he is associated.

And what book on ancient Egyptian mythology would be complete without a closer look at the god Ra. In earlier chapters, we've discussed Ra at the birth of the universe and his role in some traditions as its progenitor, but the daily travels of the sun-god are of particular importance here, as they were to the ancient Egyptians themselves; that being so, I'll take you on a journey of one day and night with Ra.

The morning begins with Ra being birthed from Nut, the sky goddess and swallowing up all of the stars (and in some traditions, all of the gods) as he does. In this earliest stage, he is often represented by the scarab Khephra, a symbol of rebirth to the Egyptians. In this stage, he is often called Ra-Horakhty, a union of the gods Ra and Horus. With the beginning of his travels, the world becomes revitalized and life again rises on the face of the earth. He begins to make his way through the sky, becoming stronger as he approaches the midpoint of the sun (noon,) but along the way, he is often beset by many challenges. One of the harshest trials that Ra endures as he makes his way through the sky is undergoing assault by Apep, the god of disorder and destruction. As he is beset by his daily foe, he is aided in his battles by those who travel with him (usually Thoth and Ma'at,) and he overcomes the chaos and is able to continue his journey.

By midday, he has reached the height of his power and strength. For a moment, he is the perfect idea of the virile god, whose creative force and life-giving energy refreshes and revitalizes the world, but from this point on, he begins to age. As he continues his travels, he grows older and older until, at sunset, he becomes the god Atum, the oldest god and their creator. When this happens, he enters into the mouth of Nut and spits out all of the stars (and gods,) but his journey is hardly over.

As he travels through the body of Nut, he is also travelling through the duat, the Egyptian underworld. As he comes across the souls of the dead, those whose hearts were devoured are burned in pits of fire and tormented; while those who passed the test of Ma'at are invigorated and renewed. As he reaches the midpoint of his passage through the body of Nut (midnight) he comes upon Osiris, the god of the dead. The two join, forming the constancy (Osiris) and progression (Ra) of time, life and, indeed, all things. As you may remember, Osiris is known for his ability to resurrect and rejuvenate and thus, upon their meeting, Ra becomes invigorated again, and is able to resume his journey.

He moves onward and through the remainder of the body of Nut, finally being reborn through her, and a new day rises as he again swallows the stars.

This conception of the travels of Ra informs us greatly on the Egyptian's ideas concerning astronomical events, specifically solar motion and where the stars come from at night and where they go during the day. Without the travels of Ra, life would not be able to exist. Thus, as a solar god, Ra is another example of a deity who "dies" and is "reborn" in order to bring life to the world. This can be seen in many different traditions, including Greek and Roman mythologies.

The pantheon certainly doesn't end with our next goddess, but it wouldn't be complete without Nephthys. We've discussed the role of Nephthys as the consort of Set and the sister of Isis who helped with the finding of Osiris's remains, however, there is more to this goddess than just those simple attributions.

Nephthys was the goddess of death and lamentation, but also, at times, seen as a celebratory figure. In the Egyptian conception of death, the deceased would be granted the strength to proceed through their trials through the combined influence of Isis and Nephthys. She was a protector of the dead and often described as "the nursing mother." In many myths, she takes a particularly intimate role in the rearing of the young Horus before he grew to adulthood and his seat of power.

Nephthys could usually be seen (generally along with her sister, Isis) in Egyptian depictions of death-scenes, or representations of the underworld. She may have been a figure of death to the Egyptians, but she was generally revered among them.

It's difficult to know where to begin or end a chapter on the specific gods and goddesses of Egypt. For instance, in the mythology, without the god Khnemu, a drought of seven years wouldn't have been ended. Without Heh, there would be no infinity. Without Amun-Ra, the Theban patron god (Amun) may never have nearly taken over the entire pantheon of the

Egyptian belief system. Okay, Amun had a little help from the pharaohs, but the fact remains that it is impossible to overstate the importance to each of the gods and goddesses, however minor they may appear throughout the entirety of the Egyptian system.

Not only were there so many individual gods, there were so many combinations thereof that had importance to the Egyptians that only delving deeper into a few is–while necessary–unfortunate. Different gods would rise and fall in power and influence as the power and the influence of their patron cities rose and fell.

There are countless numbers of primary sources in the forms of scrolls, etchings, statuary and burial items from which we gain more information about the gods and their duties and attributions; in many cases, these differ from one another, sometimes vastly. I encourage you to delve deeper into these, should you have the time and interest, and see the treasures which can be found within.

CHAPTER 12

Two Tales of the Ancients

Not all parts of Egyptian mythology and/or religion regarded the gods directly. Many of the myths of the ancient Egyptians were tales of morality, of triumph and loss, love and warfare, and it is in this chapter that we will take a closer look at those. Some are somewhat strange to us today, but others have a striking resemblance to stories that we still tell today.

Due to the necessary length of these stories, I am only able to include a very select number of them, but I think these particular tales can give you an idea of the character of the Egyptian thought in a couple of very specific ways.

Let's begin with the tale of The Prince and the Sphinx. This is the story from "The Dream Stelé" of Thutmose IV, the pharaoh who rediscovered and unburied the great sphinx. This story would be used by Thutmose IV himself as a way to grant a sort of ideological legitimacy to his claim to the throne of Egypt.

Thutmose, a prince of Egypt was born to the pharaoh Amenhotep. He was only one of a number of siblings (and thus, possible heirs,) but he was being groomed to be pharaoh, much to the chagrin of his envious brothers and sisters. As in most stories of this type, the wicked siblings would often try to make Thutmose look bad in front of both his father and the others who might have a say in his ability to lead Egypt. Often these were simple lies, stating that he lacked discretion or balance, that he did not revere the gods enough or properly, but as time went on, the actions of his siblings became more and more drastic, and it was beginning to look like he may not be made pharaoh after all.

Thutmose was a skilled archer and, indeed, quite talented in every way which a young pharaoh-to-be could want to be, but the vitriol of his siblings drove him not only to unhappiness, but to escape the royal palace whenever he could. He would present himself when called upon, but was notorious for absconding at the first opportunity.

One of his greatest loves was to hunt with his bow at the cusp of the desert where he could be alone and ply his skills. As a skilled charioteer, he would chase his game. It is said that his were the fastest horses in the kingdom, and he often used his chariot in his hunting expeditions.

While a festival was being held at the royal palace, Thutmose decided to leave on a hunting trip once more, taking a couple of his servants along with him. They hunted far and long and the desert eventually began to grow too hot to continue. Still restless, Thutmose continued on, finally coming across the enormous stone head of a pharaoh protruding from the sand, buried to the neck. Thutmose finally collapsed from exhaustion and fell asleep beneath this enormous stone figure.

When he awoke, he found himself still under the sphinx, but no longer felt alone. It is then that the sphinx spoke to him. It told him that his heirship would be ensured, if only the young prince would remove the sand covering the rest of its figure. Thutmose was skeptical at first, due to the efficacy of his siblings' smear campaigns against him, but did as the sphinx had instructed and revealed the body of the lion to which the head of the pharaoh was attached. Upon his return to the royal palace, Thutmose was granted Pharaohship of Egypt.

The original version of the preceding story was found when the sphinx was uncovered, yet again, after having been buried up to the neck in sand. The stelé containing this story was directly between the forepaws of the sphinx itself. This story gives us an idea how mythologies and propaganda were often used by pharaohs to garner public favor and to legitimize their rule and/or their actions.

Next we'll take a look at one of the much later myths of Egypt, and gives an idea of the changes which were occurring in the land shortly before the Persians conquered the land. This tale was actually originally penned by Herodotus, a Greek, and was likely told to him as he travelled in the land of Egypt. The reason for including a partially Grecian story here is that it gives us an idea of the impact of Greece on Egypt just before the fall of the great pharaohs. There are a few names in here that you may recognize. This particular tale bears quite a resemblance to a more modern fairy tale. Let's see if you can figure out which one...

A short time before Egypt would be taken by the Persian Empire, there was a pharaoh named Ahmose II. During this time, the threat of the Persians was constantly growing and, in an effort to ward off invasion, Ahmose welcomed trade and immigration from Greece, even going as far as to give them their own city, thus giving Greece a stake in the fate of Egypt.

During this time, the slave trade was big business, and a Grecian, said to be the brother of Sappho, was walking through town. He had been a tradesman for many years and had accumulated a great deal of wealth. His name was Charaxos.

One day, as Gharaxos was walking through the marketplace, he noticed a large group gathered and decided to investigate. What he came upon was a slave being sold, obviously a Grecian woman. When Charaxos saw this woman, he was instantly struck by her beauty and decided that he must be the one to buy her.

Being quite well off from his years as a merchant and tradesman, he was able to purchase the woman with ease. Upon collecting his purchase, he inquired as to the woman's name. She told him that she was called Rhodopis, and that she had become a slave after having been captured by privateers when she was a child. She had been sold to a wealthy man who had many other slaves besides her. In time, she became close friends with a ragged, ugly old slave by the name of Aesop who had told her countless marvelous tales. It is through this old man's stories that the girl was able to bear the burden of slavery.

By the time she had grown to womanhood, however, her master saw the potential in selling Rhodopis, due to her entrancing beauty.

Charaxos, mesmerized by the young woman's beauty and broken-hearted to hear of the hardships that she had endured immediately whisked her away. He provided her a home of her own and slaves to attend to her every whim. No expense was spared on the young woman, and she was given a secluded garden containing a pool in which to soothe herself. One of the most precious gifts that the old man bestowed upon this woman, who he saw as a daughter, was a pair of slippers, the color of a red rose.

She lay one day in her pool, bathing herself while her personal slaves attended to her belongings. The sun was beating down heavily, but the young woman couldn't have been more content as she lazed in the cool waters within her secluded garden.

Just as she had reached the pinnacle of relaxation, a furor was heard coming from the slave girls. An eagle had descended upon them and they ran screaming from the pool, leaving Rhodopis's clothing and jewelry behind. Rhodopis, hearing the commotion, backed against the edge of her pool as her slaves hid, fearing the eagle was going to attack them.

The eagle, however, wasn't after the girls.

With a single swoop, it snatched one of the red slippers in its talons and took off again into the sky from whence it came. Rhodopis, having loved the slipper and, indeed, all of the gifts which her new benefactor had bestowed upon her, wept, saddened by the loss of her beautiful gift.

The eagle, however, (one of the symbols of the god Horus) had been sent forth with a specific purpose and it travelled, still carrying the slipper, all the way to the seat of the Egyptian pharaoh, Ahmose II.

The pharaoh was attending to his duties, arbitrating disputes among his people when the eagle soared in and dropped the slipper onto the lap of the pharaoh. The pharaoh was enamored with the fine workmanship of the slipper and became convinced that such a lavish adornment could only belong to the most beautiful woman in the world.

So taken was he that he gathered his servants and bade them go to every nome (city) in Egypt with the red slipper and declare the woman whose foot it fit that she would be his wife.

The servants and messengers went far and wide, taking the slipper with them everywhere they went, but alas, the shoe was too small to fit any of the women who claimed it to be theirs.

It wasn't until they happened upon the city of Naucratis that they were informed of the merchant and the beautiful slave-girl that he had purchased. The tales of the lavish gifts that he showered upon her sent the servants running. Upon their arrival, Rhodopis was by the very pool where her slipper had been taken. When they caught her attention, she immediately recognized the slipper and cried out in joy. She sent one of her slaves to retrieve the mate of the slipper to prove her ownership of the pair, and the messengers were convinced.

They informed her that the pharaoh had commanded them to find the woman to whom the slipper belonged and return her to his palace where she would be given a place of honor and that it was the god Horus himself who had sent him on his search for her.

She said a tearful goodbye to Charaxos who, while thrilled for her gain, mourned for his own loss. She then went forth with the messengers to Memphis, the capitol of Egypt at the time and, upon seeing Rhodopis, the pharaoh knew her to be the woman for whom he had been searching.

The words of the messengers were fulfilled and exceeded as she was not only given high honor, but made the queen of the pharaoh. The two would live in delirious happiness until one year before the invasion of the Persians. They died together with Egypt still intact.

Okay, so if you haven't guessed, that story is the origin of Cinderella. Written many centuries before the brothers Grimm would augment the tale to the form from which our modern retelling is based.

In the tales of the Egyptians, we can often see the origin of the stories that we tell each other today. The Egyptians were, in truth, not all that different from us, at least not on a human level. Their civilization was based upon different structures and their religious beliefs may differ from those of the modern world in ways, but at the heart of Egyptian mythology there is a soul which resonates with us still. We want the same things that we wanted back then: love, respect, honor; and we still have the same fears and strikingly similar ways of dealing with them. To share our experiences, we tell stories as the Egyptians did. It is what makes these stories timeless, this constancy of the human spirit: often troubled, but perpetually looking for that next ray of light to shine down and change our lives.

Martin R. Phillips

CHAPTER 13

Monuments and the Parts of the Soul

The juxtaposition between the two halves of the title may seem strange at first, but they are indelibly linked with one another. To the ancient Egyptians, there were five parts of the soul: the Ka, the Ba, the Sheut, the Ren and the Ib. Each of these parts played a role not only in a person's ha (or body) or their spiritual experience, but had a great deal to do with why the Egyptian architecture was the way that it was.

As has been mentioned in an earlier chapter, bringing form to something through writing or carving wasn't just an active action with a passive result, it was at all times active. That is to say that when something was created through even artistic media, it was thought to have been brought forth into the world as a concept that lived and shaped the world around it for its presence. Therefore, the retelling of a story, in the minds of the Egyptians, literally caused the story to happen again. That is why there is no particularly detailed description of the death of Osiris: the Egyptians didn't want to bring that calamity forth again. Perhaps the belief didn't go quite so far as that, perhaps it did, but what we have is what we were left and, although new discoveries are constantly being made in Kemet (the Egyptians' name for Egypt, meaning Black Land,) structures, whether they were for artistic purposes or practical ones served more than their simple function to the Egyptians.

This concept is most notable in regard to the Ka. The Ka is the part of the soul that is basically the breath of life; that which differentiates a live person with a dead one. It can be related to the spirit, and was believed to be breathed into every living person at the moment of their birth by either Meskhenet or Heqet, depending on the locale. For those of significant power or wealth, particularly pharaohs, Ka Statues were created in their likeness in order to provide a place for their Ka, or essence of vitality to live on after their death in this plane.

This aspect of a person's soul would wander freely over the face of existence, but could only have a permanent home through a body. This is the reason for the Ka Statues. These can be most easily identified by a pair of upraised arms placed atop the head of the statue. This is the symbol of the Ka. Ka Statues, like other statuary depicting people, face directly forward so that the Ka can have an unobstructed view of the world around, although the Ka would technically be part of that which existed within the other realm, through Ka Statues, it could have an earthly seat as well.

The other aspects of the soul (the Ba, the Ren, the Ib and the Sheut) can be described as follows, starting with the Ba:

The Ba can be best described as the individuality or the personality of a person or an object; basically, that which makes one different from any other. A work of art could certainly be said to have a ba, just as a person did. Have you ever noticed a particular attachment that you may have to a particular thing due to its unique character or its sentimental value? This could be said to be one aspect of that thing's Ba.

The more important aspect of the Ba to the Egyptians was that it was the specific essence of an individual that would live on after their death. It was symbolized in hieroglyph by a bird with a human's head. The Ba could also be referred to as a representation of this principle as the pyramids of Egypt were also referred to as the Ba of Khufu or Sneferu, etc.

The Ren was a person's name. It was that which would be applied upon the birth of a child, but would not die so long as it continued to be spoken or written. The latter aspect of this can be related to the phrase, "[person's name] lives on in our memories," and to the Egyptians, this was a very real thing. So long as a person's Ren was to be spoken and/or preserved, it would live on. This being the case, those who were celebrated had their names written all over the land to ensure their Ren's survival. Conversely, if a person was despised, or fell out of favor, it wasn't uncommon for their name to be literally removed from all known records.

The Ib is something which we have discussed, although only once by name so far. The Ib is the heart of the individual. The Ib doesn't only represent the physical organ, but certain principles as well; such as the thoughts, the will, the objectives and passions of the person. The Ib, which comes into being at the conception of the child through a single drop of its mother's own heart, would stand as to the nature of the individual and that which they carried with them throughout their life. This is why it is the Ib, or the heart that is weighed by Anubis against the weight of Ma'at's feather. The expression, "It is with a heavy heart…" may or may not have originated in Egypt (probably not,) but it would certainly indicate something very specific to the Egyptian mind. In contrast, the expression "light-hearted" (again, probably not of Egyptian origin etymologically) would also have a celebratory air to it to an Egytpian.

The Sheut, or šwt is the shadow of a person. Due to its omnipresence about a person (at night, it would simply blend with the darkness,) it was believed to be a representation and a crucial part of that person. The Sheut carried certain aspects of an individual. In fact, the term "shadow box," when used to describe a box for storing something of particular worth actually originates with this concept as many of the pharaohs actually had boxes made in order to contain portions of their Sheuts. The Sheut wasn't one of the parts of the soul generally preserved (or attempted/thought to be preserved) after a person's death, unless it was through use of a Sheut Box or statuary, however, it was still considered to be a necessary and important part of the person's soul.

During life, all of these parts of the soul resided with the body whether inside (as the Ka, Ba and Ib,) outside (as in the Sheut,) or metaphorically carried by the individual (as in the case of the Ren.) Upon death, each had their place and their direction, in short, their purpose to the continuation of the life of the person beyond the grave.

Many of the monuments of Egypt are in some way connected with one or more portions of the soul. As it has been discussed, the ba could be likened to the pyramids, especially those of more distinct structure such as those of Khufu and Sneferu, but what else did the pyramids symbolize to the Egyptians?

The pyramids were burial chambers. This much is definitely true. It was in the pyramids that the bodies and the offerings to their Kas (as the Ka was seen to be the part of the person which required sustenance such as food or water) were stored, but what else did these structures mean to the Egyptians? Is there a reason behind the specific shape of the pyramids? Were the pyramids built by aliens? How about I stop asking questions and start giving answers?

First off, there is no evidence to suggest that aliens built the pyramids. However, there is also no evidence to suggest that they were built by slaves either. The pyramids were most likely constructed by paid laborers at the behest of their pharaoh.

Rather than focus on the material essence of the pyramids, however, let's focus on the spiritual significance of them.

The shape of the pyramids represents that of the first bit of land to come forth out of the waters of Nanuet. Being the first shape which was brought forth out of these waters holds a number of different meanings, all of which could be said to apply to the pyramids themselves. Structure out of chaos: in the case of Benben (the first bit of land,) it was land out of the chaos; in the case of the pyramids, it was a permanent structure ensuring that those interned within would not be simply cast to the winds. Another possible parallel is that of moving from one plane of existence to another: in the case of Benben, it was the formation of the earth itself; in the case of the pyramids, it symbolizes the journey from the land of the living to the land of the dead.

The pyramids are, and have long been, a symbol of strength and permanence, and it can't be ruled out that that was a possible motivation as well. We may never know the reason behind every nuance of these magnificent structures, however, as time goes on, we are discovering more and more about the land, its people and their beliefs. I think it's probable that we may just learn a lot more about the pyramids as Ra continues his journeys through the sky.

The structures of the ancient Egyptians were more than mere edifices or artistic representations of people or concepts, to the Egyptians; they were living, vibrant things with a life of their own. The parts of the soul were represented throughout the world of ancient Egypt, often preserved, sometimes scratched out, but always a part of that magnificent world.

CONCLUSION

Of the numerous inscriptions, papyri, carvings and artefacts that have been uncovered, so it seems that more questions arise regarding the mythology of the ancient Egyptians. For a moment, there will be something akin to ultimate clarity, only to be muddled by contradiction or the sheer incompleteness of our present knowledge of this vast and powerful society.

Within the Egyptian religion, many gods do battle with one another; not only within the myths themselves, but through the actions of the people, replacing one with another or merging two into a new form, making a previous version of a concept obsolete. In a way, the mythology of the ancient Egyptians can be said to be like the method of science. At any given point, we have a certain understanding of things, but when we receive new information, there isn't a single thing that can't be disputed. So it was with the gods of the Egyptians.

Worshipped far and wide with temples to various deities, the gods of the Egyptians were truly a powerful force in the lives of the ancients, and they continue to influence us today. One thing that I keep coming back to, the more that I learn about Egypt though is the fact that with every new answer, there are a dozen more questions to ask. There is never that sense of completeness or the satisfaction that it's understood well enough. There's always that feeling that there is more. And there is.

The more that we respectfully uncover the past, the more that we can understand it, and hopefully the more answers we can find. For now, all that we can do is keep searching, keep delving into the ways of ancient thought. There are many improvements that we have made to our world, but there is much that we can learn from the ancient Egyptians' beliefs. Wouldn't the world be such a better place if there were to be a true sense of Ma'at? Some sort of balance where we could all thrive without destroying one another and the world that we live in?

One day, hopefully a very long time from now, the archaeologists of the future will be asking questions about us and our civilization, and I can't help but wonder: will they have more questions than answers the way that we do with the Egyptians? That, of course, is impossible to say, but interesting to speculate.

From the myth of creation to the path to the underworld, there is so much to learn about the beliefs of these peoples. Everything had a function, a specific purpose, a cause and an effect. There were often multiple gods for the same concept, and more explanations for some things than could ever be fully cohered. And yet still... there are so many questions.

I have greatly enjoyed bringing you this brief glimpse into the magical world of ancient Egyptian mythology, and I hope that you have enjoyed reading it. Check out the other books in this series, including: Discovering Ancient Egypt, Discovering Ancient Greece and Discovering Ancient Mythology.

Again, it has been an absolute pleasure to share some of the fascinating world of the ancient Egyptians with you. I hope you happy reading, and a continued thirst for history!

PART 3
NORSE
MYTHOLOGY

Ancient Secrets of the Norse

INTRODUCTION

The religion of the Norse or, as they referred to it, Tradition, has captured the minds of many. Though the religion and beliefs of the Vikings are largely out of practice in the world today, the influence of this religion lives on, and in a very profound way.

In the modern day, we see Norse mythos cropping up in movies, television and anime, as well as video games such as Final Fantasy VII, and in comic books. This interest has also reached into the world of music, both from indigenous genres such as the black metal of Norway and other Scandinavian countries, but can be found in various other forms of music and artistic expression.

But what *did* the Norse believe? How did they view the world and what was their conception of their gods? In this book, it is my aim to give you, the reader, an overview of Norse mythology in a way that's not only informative, but interesting.

As with my other texts on mythology (Greek Mythology and Egyptian Mythology) I've found the most effective way to communicate the stories and religion of the Norse is through their stories.

Like many societies, much of Norse lore has been lost to the ages. However, there are a few good sources in this regard, specifically the Eddas. The Poetic Edda in particular is a treasure-trove of insight into the Norse belief system and, through that lens, the Norse way of life.

One thing worthy of mention here is that the central texts still extant on Norse Tradition, namely, the Poetic Edda and the Prose Edda, were written in the thirteenth century. The Tradition, however, was around long before that. As this is the case, much of the knowledge that we now have of the Norse is incomplete and, in some cases, the Poetic Edda disagrees with the Prose Edda. The Poetic Edda, as mentioned above, is particularly insightful, however, as it collects and shares many of the stories of the Norse people.

While this book is not a complete record of the Norse beliefs (and such a record is, to my knowledge, nonexistent,) it has been my pleasure to assemble some of the most pertinent and interesting myths of the Norse. We'll find Odin on his many quests for knowledge and wisdom, the formation of the world out of the body of a giant and we even find Thor in a veiled wedding dress (no, seriously.) From the birth of the sun and moon to the berserkers of Valhalla to the eventual destruction and reformation of the nine worlds, the Norse Tradition tells of captivating gods and goddesses, of heroes and unmitigated disasters.

The pantheon of the Norse is large, like that of the Greeks, Romans and Egyptians. While some principal players such as Odin, Thor and Loki are well-fixed in the popular mindset, many others exist which are just as compelling. The Tradition of the Norse is filled with stories of valor and treachery, love and hatred, Valhalla and Hel. So, from the creation of the cosmos, according to the Norse, all the way through Ragnarök and beyond, I invite you to share this fascinating journey with me into one of the most iconic cultures the world has ever known.

CHAPTER 14

Creation of the Cosmos, the World, and the Gods

It is first necessary to point out that, unlike most creation myths, in the Norse Religion—simply referred
to by its adherents of old as "the tradition"—the creation of the cosmos and the destruction thereof was
not a one-time deal. After Ragnarök, that is, the
apocalyptic war in which many of the gods would be
killed, the world would begin anew. I mention this
here, because there are certain aspects of Ragnarök
which are good to know throughout the creation
myth, as it's something that the deities, demigods,
etc. were aware of from the beginning. Ragnarök itself will be discussed in more detail later.

According to the Norse Tradition, the primordial universe was called Ginnungagap, the void (trans. gap-
ing void.) Here, neither darkness nor light nor sound
nor silence existed. Ginnungagap was immeasurably
vast, said to extend in all directions infinitely (although, tradition also says that it was large enough
to encompass a billion universes, had they existed.
Either way, it was big—really, really big.)

From this primeval state of ultimately vast nothing-ness came two realms: Niflheimr ("house of mists,") the realm of ice, located in the north, and Muspel-heimr (alternatively, Muspell; "home of desolation") the realm of fire located in the south of Ginnunga-gap.

Muspelheimr was a realm of eternally erupting vol-canoes, thick, black smoke and flame. Winds blew smoke and volcanic exhaust throughout this realm. Muspelheimr was inhabited by the jötunn[1], Surtr, a fire-demon who wielded a sword of unmeasurable power in preparation for Ragnarök—more on him later.

Niflheimr was the land of ice and freezing rain. Just as vast and extreme a realm as Muspelheimr, Nifl-heimr was also home to unyielding winds, which blew frozen precipitation throughout its area. Nifl-heimr was also home to Hvergelmir, the primordial river (trans. bubbling/boiling spring,) and Élivágar, the primordial spring (trans. waves of ice.) From these sources, all of the waters in existence would come.

---

[1] *Plural: Jötnar. Translation/Definition: Devourer. Jötunn is often angli-cized into "giant." Although the latter attribution is accurate to a point, it does tend to leave out the spirit of the Jötnar as "devourers of worlds," and so will be used sparingly within this text.*

Although the realms of Niflheimr and Muspelheimr were, initially, separate, over time, they both spread. It is where these forces of fire and ice would meet that is of primary concern to the tale.

Once the frigid materials of Niflheimr came into contact with the molten substances of Muspelheimr, a violent reaction occurred. The waters were thrown into the air, only to fall and mix with the incredibly hot elements below. From this process, the first of the jötnar was created. The jötunn was named Ymir (also referred to as Aurgelmir.)

The mixing of the fire and lava of Muspelheimr would continue to mix with the ice and water of Niflheimr, slowly melting that which was frozen and solidifying that which was molten.

Unlike most creation myths, Ymir, the first lifeform (other than Surtr, who seemed to spring out of the fires of Muspelheimr instantaneously,) laid without life for millennia. During this time, the composition of Ymir's body continued to form and mix together.

As Ymir's composition became more stable, he began to perspire. This perspiration formed the first of his children: a male and a female. After his feet mated with each other (now there's a mental picture,) another offspring was produced: a male, six-headed jötunn. These jötnar would become the progenitors of the gods.

Now, at the same time that Ymir was forming, and the ice and snow of Niflheimr melted from the heat of the lava and fire of Muspelheimr, another being came into existence: Auðumbla, a cow. Auðumbla, who received her nourishment through salt contained within the ice, would be the source of food for Ymir who suckled from the cow's teats.

As Auðumbla continued licking her way through the frozen-but-melting expanse, she began to lick the stones beneath the ice into the shape of a man; the first of the Aesir (also, Æsir) Gods: Buri. (Alternatively, some versions have her simply uncovering the already-formed god.)

From these beginnings, the ingredients and chief movers that would go on to create the gods, the worlds (all nine of them; more on that later) and all living things, were all present.

Now for a little genealogy (I'll try to keep it brief): Buri produced a son named Bor. Bolthorn, a jötunn, produced a daughter named Bestla. Bor and Bestla would marry and give birth to the Aesir gods Odin (aka Wodan, Woden, or Wotan,) Vili and Ve (or Vé.)

Theories diverge on what led to the confrontation which led to the death of Ymir at the hands of Odin and his siblings (some say that it was a matter of usurpation, others, a noise complaint levied against the jötunn that got a little out of hand,) however, the result is the same. The blood of the slain jötunn was so vast that it would end up drowning all but one frost ogre (a type of jötunn.) The surviving frost ogre, Bergelmir, survived by climbing into a boat called a lur (alternately, by swimming through the blood, towing his wife behind by the latter's hair.)

After killing Ymir, the three used different parts of the jötunn's body to create existence as the Norse saw it: The blood of Ymir was used to create the oceans, his flesh became the soil and primary substance of the earth, stones were fashioned from his teeth, trees from his hair, mountains from his bones, the sky from his skull and the clouds from his brains.

The sky was held aloft by four dwarves[2] named Nordri, Sudri, Austri, and Vestri[3]. Embers from Muspelheimr continued to float through the air, and so the three gods collected these and placed them in the skies to light the world.

The first humans were fashioned by Odin, Vili and Ve out of driftwood. The three gods bestowed upon humans gifts: Odin breathed life into them, Vili gave

---

[2] *The dwarves began life as maggots which grew within the slain body of Ymir. With the gift of knowledge and understanding by the gods to the dwarves, they would become the master smiths and hearty creatures which are often referenced in popular culture.*

[3] *If those names sound strangely familiar, but you're having a little trouble figuring out why, here's your answer: Nordri = North, Sudri = South, Austri = East and Vestri = West.*

them knowledge and Ve gave them their physical appearance and their senses. These humans were named Askr (or Ask) and Embla.

The world of mankind, created of the slain jötunn's body, was called Midgardr (or Midgard.) This land, though surrounded by the realm of giants (the Jötnar,) was protected by the three Aesirs by fashioning a fence from the jötunn's eyelashes.

Midgard was located between the primeval realms of Niflheimr and Muspelheimr. The other eight worlds were generally invisible to the inhabitants of Midgard, although there were times where other worlds could be perceived. One example of this is the connection between Midgard and Ásgardr (or Asgard,) the world of the gods, by a "rainbow bridge" called Bifrost.

So, we now have the world of the humans. As the other eight will be discussed to varying degrees later in the book, I'll forego a close inspection of each here. However, it is helpful to know what each of these worlds were and which beings would call them home. They are as follows:

Midgard was the world of humans.
Ásgardr was the world of the Aesir gods.
Vanaheimr was the world of the Vanir gods.
Jötunheimr was the world of the Jötnar.

Álfheimr[4] was the world of the elves.
Hel was the world of the dead or Náir[5].
Svartálfar was the world of the Dvergar or dwarves.
Niflheimr was the world of ice.
Muspelheimr was the world of fire and lava, home to Surtr.

Now, the stage is set. In the next chapter, we'll take a look at the major gods of Norse Tradition, and some of the important myths surrounding them.

---

[4] *Also called Ljosalfheimr, meaning "home of the light elves."*

[5] *Specifically, the evil, dishonored or unfit dead, as Valhalla—located within the realm of Asgard—was home to the honored dead. Think of Hel as we would think of hell; after all, it's the linguistic origin of the word.*

Martin R. Phillips

CHAPTER 15

The Aesir-Vanir War and the Mead of Poetry

The Aesir-Vanir War

Although the Norse Tradition was home to a large and rather diverse group of gods and other beings, two groups of gods, the Aesir and the Vanir, through their battle and subsequent armistice would change the landscape of the pantheon.

It all starts with a woman named Gullveig. Gullveig was a völva[6] and a practitioner of seidr (also called seid or seiðr,) a type of sorcery which was primarily in practice before the Christianization of modern-day Scandinavia. Seidr, while having many facets (most infamously a type of sex-magic,) was largely concerned with the divination and subsequent alteration of destiny.

The story begins with Gullveig making her way from place to place, world to world, plying her trade for the benefit (and gold) of various groups and individ-

---

[6] This is usually translated as "carrier of a wand" or similar.

uals. When she[7] reached Asgard, home of the Aesirs, she was an instant hit with the gods.

What happened next is fairly consistent throughout different sources, but the reasoning behind it is unclear; although there are a few theories.

In one version of the tale, the Aesirian gods, Odin in particular, are angered by the seeress's admonitions regarding the power structure chosen by the Aesirs. Gullveig, being favored by the Vanirs, was to the Aesirs, a representative of those gods.

In a similar version, the main cause of conflict was that the Aesirs had become (or had simply always been) the sole recipients of the tributes paid the gods by mankind, and it was the advice of the seeress that they, the Aesirs, either pay tribute to the Vanirs, or allow a portion of the tribute to go to the same.

In yet another version, the seeress is actually the goddess Freya, who, being a practitioner and goddess of seidr, herself, had so impressed the court of the Aesirs that the latter found themselves disgusted with their own greed and willingness to subvert their laws and loyalties. They blamed the seeress for their own lust for the power which they desired for its potential to empower them. While this particular version may

---

7 Commonly, she used the name "Gullveig Heidr," which roughly translates to "gleaming one" or "bright one."

explain the connection between the Vanirs and the seeress, it's not consistent with the Eddas.

Whatever the reason was, Odin shot his spear forth, striking, but not killing or inflicting permanent injury upon the woman. In their fury, the Aesirian gods stabbed the woman with their spears and burnt her alive not once, not twice, but three times. Each time, Gullveig would resurrect from the ashes. This did not make the Aesirians happy.

When they couldn't kill the seeress, tensions began to build between the two groups of gods. At first, the Vanirs and the Aesirs tried to work out a diplomatic solution, but this ended in an impasse. The war itself isn't explained in much detail, although, commonly, it's stated that neither group could win definitive victory against the other. While the Aesirs fought by more conventional means, the Vanirs used sorcery and subterfuge as their method of attack.

It finally became apparent that neither group was likely to ever triumph over the other. So, they came together to forge a truce. It is with the truce and that which followed it that the Eddas were concerned.

The Prose Edda explains that, as a traditional show of unity and peace between the Aesirs and Vanirs, the two groups met and took turns spitting into a cauldron or vat. One of the things about the substances (even something as seemingly insignificant as saliva) of gods is that they're never mundane.

Rather than simply dumping out the vat and possibly offending one another, they decided to put the swishing fluid to good use. Therefore, from their intermingling saliva, they created a man named Kvasir.

Kvasir and the Mead of Poetry

Now, being created from god-spit may not sound like the most promising of beginnings, but Kvasir was considered as quite possibly the wisest being (certainly the wisest human) in creation. It was written that there was no question for which he couldn't provide an insightful, practical answer.

The Aesirs and Vanirs had learned their lesson about trying to take from or overthrow one another, and so Kvasir was allowed to roam freely. He travelled throughout Midgard, spreading knowledge and wisdom to all that he met.

One day, he came across two dwarves: Fjalar and Galar. These dwarves were, unbeknownst to the Kvasir, quite the murderous, anti-intellectual beings. They quickly killed Kvasir and collected his blood. As he was so endowed with wisdom, this virtue remained within his vital fluid. The two boiled it in the magic cauldron Odhrorir, and mixed it with honey (alternately, they enlist the giant Suttungr to add the nectar to the blood.) When approached about the fate of Kvasir, the dwarves said that he had choked (or suffocated) on his own intelligence. For two beings that harbored such distaste for intelligence and knowledge, the reply was really quite clever.

The mixture of blood and honey became "The Mead of Poetry." Any who would drink of the fluid would gain the knowledge and understanding to become a poet or a scholar. This was safe enough in the hands of the dwarves, as, due to their anti-intellectualism, they didn't have the desire to partake of it. However, it would be their lust for killing that would take the Mead of Poetry from their hands.

When the two decided that killing the wisest man hadn't properly slaked their bloodlust, they went before the giant Gilling and offered to take him for a ride on their boat. (It must have been a rather large vessel.) Once at sea, the murderous pair capsized the boat and watched as Gilling drowned in the depths of the ocean.

As an act of anything but contrition, the two returned to the home of Gilling and informed his wife of her husband's death. While Fjalar offered to take Gilling's wife to visit the spot of her husband's death (no doubt to dump her in the same spot,) Galar was growing weary of the wife's sobbing. The second voyage was scrapped and the dwarves simply dispatched Gilling's wife as she passed through the doorway of her home by dropping a millstone on her head.

The two psychotic dwarves rejoiced, but their mirth would be short-lived. For when Suttungr (a son of the murdered couple. Although not necessarily relevant to the rest of the story, he was rather drunk at the time. Alcohol and the ensuing drunkenness thereof was a fairly common occurrence in the stories of Norse Mythology) found out, he tracked the pair down and snatched them. He took them to a reef at low tide, with the full intention of letting the two drown in the very waters in which his father had.

The two dwarves, seeing Hel in their immediate future, quickly offered the jötunn the Mead of Poetry in exchange for their lives. Suttungr took the mead back to his home, the mountain Hnitbjörg, and placed it under the watchful eye of his daughter, Gunnlöd.

Odin

While there will be a great deal more about Odin throughout this book, as he was the chief deity of the Aesirs, he does play yet another role in the story of the Mead of Poetry.

Odin, along with being the chief deity of the Aesirs, was also a god of knowledge, royalty, berserker fury, battle, death, the arts (specifically language: the runic alphabet and poetry,) healing and sorcery—although other attributions do exist, varying a bit from source to source. His wife was the goddess Frigg, with whom he bore Baldur (also Balder, Baldr,) Hod and Hermud; with Jord: Thor; with Rind: Váli (alternately, Valie); with the jötunn, Grid: Vidar (who would slay Fenrir the wolf, more on that later.) Odin had an eight-legged horse, Sleipnir, which was the fastest creature extant, and was capable of travelling between the nine worlds with ease.

Now, Odin was tireless when it came to the search for further knowledge and wisdom. When he became aware of the Mead of Poetry and its location within Hnitbjörg, he set out to claim it for his own. In order to do this, he employed quite the clever (if rather brutal) deception.

He began by traveling to the home of Baugi, the younger brother of Suttungr, disguised as a common farmer. Upon his arrival, he found nine farmhands tending to the fields. The god offered to sharpen the farmhands' scythes for them, and the workers agreed.

Being the chief deity of, well, pretty much everything, he was able to sharpen the farmers' scythes with such deft effectiveness that the men implored him to sell them the whetstone he had used. Odin agreed, but rather than simple trade or barter, the god tossed the whetstone into the air and, before it fell to the ground, the workers killed one another with the very scythes the deity had just sharpened.

Upon making his way to the house of Baugi, he was offered shelter for the night. While there, the jötunn shared his frustration at the mutual killing of his workers. Odin, not quite magnanimously, offered to work the fields in the farmhands' stead… for a price. The price was a sip of the mead which Baugi's brother had come to possess. The jötunn hesitantly agreed, and Odin—by this point, calling himself Bölverkr so as to not expose his true identity—set to work.

Odin worked through the summer and the fall. When winter finally came, Odin asked about his payment. He and Baugi went to Hnitbjörg to convince Suttungr to allow the gracious farmhand to wet his lips with the Mead of Poetry.

Baugi should have checked with his brother before offering some of the mead as payment, though, as Suttungr refused. Odin, being quite the persuasive type, convinced Baugi to help him reach the mead through other means, namely, by boring through the mountain and into the dwelling of Gunnlöd, the guardian of the mead.

Odin gave the jötunn a drill with which to bore through the mountain. Baugi initially tried to deceive him by only drilling partway through, but Odin discovered the ruse by blowing into the hole, causing the dust and debris to come out the top of the hole. Once the god had convinced the jötunn to fulfill his end of the bargain, he repeated his test, this time, satisfied that Baugi had, indeed followed through.

Odin changed his form into that of a snake and slithered his way through the hole. Although Baugi promptly tried to stab him with the auger, the Aesir made it through unscathed.

Once inside, Odin morphed into the figure of a young, attractive man and set to work making an arrangement with Gunnlöd. The arrangement was that if she would give him three sips of the mead, Odin would share Gunnlöd's bed for three consecutive nights. Being that Odin had turned himself into quite the handsome rogue, Gunnlöd agreed.

After three nights with Gunnlöd, Odin persisted regarding the mead. Gunnlöd took him to the chamber where the mead was stored. The draught was contained within three vessels. Odin took a drink from each, but rather than a sip, he consumed the entirety of the Mead of Poetry.

Not being one to stick around and gloat, Odin transformed himself into an eagle and flew off in the direction of Asgard. Suttungr quickly came to discover what had happened and gave chase, turning himself into an eagle. Odin would prove too fast for him, though. As the god approached Asgard, the other Aesirs saw the chase and set vats of their own along the border of the realm.

Odin quickly regurgitated the mead into the vessels, but the closing proximity of the giant forced the god to be a bit hasty. A few drops of the Mead of Poetry fell from his mouth (or, in this case, beak,) and landed in Midgard, the realm of humanity.

Suttungr retreated, as he was outnumbered. The drops which fell to Midgard were available for the consumption of any, but lacked sufficient quantity to do its full work. It's from these drops, the Norse believed, that those mediocre in poetry and/or scholarship gained their lackluster "inspiration." The rest of the Mead of Poetry, however, was doled out by Odin himself, empowering his fellow gods along with his favored poets and scholars to untold heights of genius.

Thus, what started as the first war in Norse Tradition eventually gave rise to new apexes of poetic and scholarly work. I can't help but wonder if Odin gave some of this draught to the authors of the Eddas.

CHAPTER 16

Freyja, Loki and Thor, Myths and Legends

The pantheon of Norse Mythology (Tradition) is vast, filled with gods and demigods of varying powers and temperaments. After the Vanir-Aesir War, the two camps came together and, for the most part, worked famously with one another. That said, there is plenty to learn about the deities, and thus, the Norse conception of life, the world and the cosmos.

As some of the more poignant stories regarding the individual gods are of their interactions with one another, in this chapter, it serves well to not only include stories of the individual deities, but to introduce and include other gods pertinent to their stories.

Freyja, Loki and Thor:

Freyja and the Disappearance of Óðr

Freyja (alternately, Freya,) was a Vanir, a daughter of Njord and his wife Nerthus (who was also Njord's sister.) Freya was the twin sister to Freyr. Freya was a goddess of many things, including beauty, fertility, sexuality, luxury, death and war. She was also a goddess of seidr. Her consort was Óðr (possibly an early form of the name Odin.) Her day is Fredag (Friday.)

Before her husband, Óðr left (more on that in a moment,) the two had two daughters named Hnoss and Gersemi[8]. Now, Óðr, whose name commonly translates into "the wanderer," or "the frenzied one," although many other attributions of the name do exist. Not much is generally known of Óðr himself, apart from his connection with Freyja.

One day, Óðr simply vanished. While it's unknown exactly where he went or what happened to him after he left[9], Óðr's departure had a rather profound effect on Freyja. She tried to find or follow him, weeping, along her way.

---

[8] Both names meaning "jewel" or "gem."

[9] It is, however, theorized that Óðr simply traveled from land to land, though always out of the reach of his wife.

Freyja was the most desired of the goddesses with gods, Jötnar and men. Her propensity toward lust once got her into quite the row with Loki.

Loki and the Art of Not Keeping One's Mouth Shut

Loki was the son of Fárbauti and Laufey, and brother to Helblindi and Býleistr. Some testimonies refer to him as a god, others as a jötunn[10], while others claim him as being both. He was a mischievous being, and was just as likely to hinder the gods as to help them.[11]

Now, Loki was kind of a jerk. At one gathering, thrown by the god Ægir, Loki became furious at the servants of Ægir, named Fimafeng and Eldir, for being so kind and accommodating toward the other gods, who he saw as being corrupt and unworthy of praise[12]. To make his point, Loki killed Fimafeng.

Regardless the reason for Loki's jealousy, the gods didn't stand for this act and chased him from the hall.

---

[10] Likely due to his sexual relationship with the jötunn Angrboða; the union of which produced Jörmungandr, the World Serpent (see chapter five,) the wolf Fenrir and the goddess Hel.

[11] One of the central myths of Loki is his involvement in the death of Baldur; this will be discussed in the following chapter.

[12] Or, in some versions, that Loki was infuriated by the kindness of the gods toward these servants, who he, again, saw as being unworthy of the praise.

He retreated into the woods for a time and the gods went back to their mead.

Upon his return, Loki accosted the remaining servant, Eldir. Although he left Eldir alive, the gods weren't about to allow Loki to return into the hall. In response to this, Loki invoked the oath sworn by Odin that the two would drink with one another, and Odin allowed the trickster god back to the table.

While a god with a little more humility, or at least a little more tact, may not have tried to push his luck, Loki began insulting the gods. He claimed that the gods were weak and sexually promiscuous. Freyja, being particularly offended by this, challenges Loki, saying that the latter was mad to be so vitriolic in the presence of the goddess Frigg, as Frigg knew the future and fate of all.

Loki snapped back, accusing Freyja of having lain with every god and elf in the hall[13]. The row goes on for quite some time.

Another myth involves Freyja, Loki and (let's be honest, you've been waiting for him to make an appearance,) Thor (Þórr in the original Norse.) First though, it bears telling how Thor's hammer came into existence.

---

[13] This may or may not have been an accurate accusation, given Freyja's love of, well, love.

Loki and the Creation of Thor's Hammer

Thor's iconic hammer, Mjölnir, was forged by the dwarves Brokkr and Sindri, as part of a bet with Loki. In this bet, Loki literally bet his head that the two dwarves couldn't make anything more stunning or functional than the Sons of Ivaldi—famous for such things as Odin's spear or lance, Gungir. The two were sucked into the challenge and set about constructing a hammer.

Sindri worked the forge and Brokkr, the bellows. Sindri instructed Brokkr that, under no circumstances was the latter to stop working the bellows until he (Sindri) had finished his part of the work and removed it from the forge.

Now, as already stated, Loki was kind of a jerk. During the first portion of the work, Sindri placed pig leather into the forge. As Sindri worked, Brokkr manned the bellows. All was fine until Loki turned himself into a biting fly in an attempt to get the dwarf to pause just long enough to ruin the material. Loki, as a fly, bit Brokkr hard on the hand, but the dwarf persisted in his duties.

Sindri finished his first item: A boar, Gullinbursti, which the dwarves would offer to the god Freyr. Gullinbursti was capable of running through water and air with more swiftness than any steed may, and the boar's bristles and mane were of such shimmering gold that darkness would retreat in its presence.

Next, Sindri placed gold into the forge and, again, set to work. Loki, undaunted by his previous failure to flummox Brokkr, returned again, this time biting the dwarf hard on the neck. As before, though, the dwarf didn't flinch.

When Sindri had finished, he removed the finished product from the forge: The magical ring, Draupnir, which, every ninth night, would produce eight more rings, identical in size, shape and quality. This ring, the dwarves gave to Odin.

Finally, Sindri set to work on the final artifact by placing iron into the forge. Loki again landed on Brokkr, this time biting him deeply on the eyelid. While the dwarf could withstand the pain, he stopped working the bellows for the briefest of moments as he wiped the blood from his eye.

When Sindri had finished with the third and final item, the hammer Mjölnir, the handle was shorter than intended, due to Brokkr's failure to keep the bellows going continuously. This is why Thor's hammer, despite its depictions in modern-day media, could only be wielded with one hand.

Although Loki had succeeded in getting Brokkr to stop working the forge, if only for an instant, it was clear that the dwarves had won the bet. Loki, never one to lose graciously, protested by saying that, though the two had a right to his head, in order to take it, they would have to separate it from his neck. As cutting or otherwise damaging his neck wasn't part of the bargain, Loki convinced the dwarves to leave Loki's head where it was.

That's not to say that the dwarves were happy about it. Though they were unable to take Loki's head, Brokkr—undoubtedly with some satisfaction—sewed Loki's mouth shut with wire as a lesson in not making bets that can't be paid.

The Theft of Thor's Hammer

Thor was the god of thunder, lightning and storms in general. Other attributions include him as the god of strength, the defender of humanity, healing and oak trees among others. He was the son of Odin and Jord (or Jörð; Earth.) His day is Thor's Day, or, more modernly, Thursday. He was a redhead who, despite the fact he was rather slow-witted, was fierce in battle.

After receiving his hammer from the dwarves, Thor awoke one morning to find that the weapon had gone missing. As stated before, Loki was kind of a jerk and Thor knew this. He assumed that the hammer was taken by Loki and went before the miscreant god, demanding that Mjölnir be returned.

Loki, however, persisted that he had nothing to do with the theft; although, he told Thor, he had a pretty good idea who did the deed. In order to for Loki to reach the culprit, Thor implored Freyja, asking her to let Loki borrow her cloak, made of the feathers of falcons, so that he may regain his hammer. Freyja assented, and Loki, lifted by the cloak (specifically, its ability to grant its wearer the power of flight,) travelled to Jötunheimr.

Once he'd arrived, he came across the jötunn, Thrymr (Þrymr in the original Norse.) Thrymr quickly admit-

ted to having taken the hammer and hiding it some-
where below the earth, at or around a depth of eight
miles. He was so fast to make his confession because
he wanted something in return: He wanted the most
beautiful of the goddesses as his wife. In other words,
he wanted Freyja in exchange for Thor's hammer.

Earlier in this chapter, we learned how Freyja was the
most desired of the goddesses, and was known for
"spreading the love," but she was far from being
without standards. When Loki returned to Thor with
the jötunn's demand, and Thor, subsequently, went
before Freyja to beg her to go through with the jötunn's demands, she snorted, flatly refusing to marry
the jötunn.

With Freyja unwilling to become the concubine of the
treacherous giant, the gods came together to figure
out how to get the hammer back as, without it, the
Jötnar were likely to use it to attack (and likely lay
waste) to Asgard. Heimdall, a god with nine mothers
(let that sink in for a minute,) finally suggested a
bold plan: For Thor to dress as Freyja and go before
the jötunn himself in order to retrieve his hammer.

Thor, reluctantly, agreed and was thus dressed in the
garments of Freyja, right down to her necklace and
keys. Loki, never wanting to miss out on much, decided to ride with Thor, posing as a bridesmaid.
Thrymr saw the disguised gods approaching and be-

came overwhelmed with excitement, having his servants quickly get to work preparing for the wedding.

Once at the wedding reception, Thor didn't hold his cover very well, as he devoured eight salmon, an ox (the whole ox) and enough mead to drop a detachment of Vikings. Thrymr, though rather impressed, began to grow a little suspicious. Loki explained that Freyja had been so enamored with the idea of wedding Thrymr that, in preparation for the wedding, she had fasted for eight days[14].

Thrymr finally got tired of waiting to plant a kiss on his new "bride." When he lifted the veil, the jig would have been up if it weren't for Loki's penchant for trickery. He explained "the bride's" fiery eyes by saying that she hadn't slept in eight days, also in preparation for the wedding.

Things came to a head, though, when Thrymr sets Mjölnir in Thor's lap as per his agreement with Loki. With his hammer now in hand, Thor tore his disguise asunder and slaughtered not only Thrymr, but the other jötnar who had attended the wedding.

---

[14] See Little Red Riding Hood.

CHAPTER 17

Central Myths, Legends and Stories

With so many gods and even more legends, Norse Tradition is a treasure-trove of interesting tales regarding the gods and the worlds. One of the most interesting tales is that of Odin and Mimir, and that's where this chapter begins.

Odin and Mimir

Mimir ("the wise one,") was unparalleled in his wisdom and advice, save, possibly for Kvasir. Mimir had a spring or a well, called Mimisbrunnr, which contained the waters of wisdom.

As we've seen, Odin was always on the lookout for a way to increase his knowledge and perspicacity, and so, when Mimir asked him to leave one of his eyes as payment for partaking of the waters, Odin did so, gladly.

The following are three tales of Odin and his quest for, and attainment of, wisdom.

How Mimir Lost His Head

The association of Odin and Mimir would not end there, though. After the Aesir-Vanir War, the two camps sent members of their ranks as hostages to the other in the Norse tradition. The Aesirs sent to the Vanir were Hoenir and Mimir[15][16].

---

[15] The Vanir sent Freyja, her brother Freyr and their father Njord to the Aesirs. This is how the Vanir Freyja became a member of the Aesir camp.

[16] In another version of this tale, Mimir was simply killed in the battle between the Aesirs and Vanirs. What happened after his beheading, however, generally remains consistent.

While in Vanaheim, home of the Vanirs, Hoenir quickly became regarded as a source of indomitable wisdom, or at least, that's what they thought. Hoenir was simply regurgitating the words of Mimir, but the ruse continued.

Now, while Mimir held wisdom beyond the ages, Hoenir was much less schooled. While Mimir was with Hoenir, the latter appeared to be a sage, but once Mimir had left Hoenir's side things unraveled rather quickly.

After Hoenir copped out of answering difficult questions one too many times, simply repeating, "Let others decide," the Vanir cut Mimir's head off, claiming that they'd been swindled and that the exchange of hostages hadn't been fair. To show their disapproval further, they sent Mimir's head back to the Aesirs.

Upon finding this, Odin was distraught. Mimir had been a friend and a trusted advisor to him, and so he preserved the head. Despite being decapitated, Mimir continued to offer Odin advice as a literal talking head.

Odin and the Runes

The Runic language of the Norse is fascinating. Runes were not simple pictorial or literary depictions of letters or words, but were intrinsically principles of power.

Odin was drawn to discovering these runes, but the process by which he would have to go to uncover them is right up there in self-mutilation for the sake of knowledge (if not simply humiliation with a nice payoff at the end) with the act of plucking out his own eye.

Odin, in furthering his quest for wisdom, travelled to the Well of Urd, the home of runic knowledge. The runes wouldn't just show themselves to anyone—not even a god like Odin—whoever sought them had to prove themselves worthy of their power.

In order to show his worth and his tenacity, Odin hung himself from the world tree, Yggdrasil, stabbing himself in the side with his own lance. He would remain there for nine days, turning away any offers of aid from the other gods. During this time, Odin came close to death, but managed to live long enough for the runes to reveal themselves to him; his sacrifice had been accepted.

Once in possession of the knowledge of the runes, Odin freed himself from Yggdrasil and carried his knowledge back to the gods and, subsequently, mankind.

The Battle of Wits: A Final Tale of Odin's Wisdom

While this portion of Norse lore happened after the death of Baldur (discussed later in the chapter,) it bears stating here.

Odin once set out to prove his sapience, by challenging a powerful seeress, named Vathruthnir. In order to protect his true identity, Odin donned disguise. The two would engage one another in a battle of wits[17]. As the exchange holds useful information about the Norse beliefs, a portion of this back-and-forth will be included, however briefly, here.

The seeress began the questioning, by asking Odin the names of the horses that drew the day and the night, respectively through the sky. Odin answered that the horses were Hrimfaxi, the drawer of the night; while Skinfaxi pulled the day.

Odin then asked Vathruthnir about the origins of the sun and the moon. To this, the seeress correctly responded that they were the children of the jötunn, Mundilfäri. The daughter, Sól, pulled the sun while Máni, Mundilfäri's son, drove the moon.

The two went back and forth for quite some time, each proving worthy in their knowledge of the worlds and its inhabitants.

---

[17] In some tellings, the loser of the bout would be killed.

It wasn't until Gagnráðr asked the seeress what Odin said to his son Baldur before setting him adrift in the Norse funerary tradition   that his cover was blown.

Vathruthnir concluded that the only one who would know the answer to that would be Odin, but conceded that the latter had proven his superior wisdom.

The Tale of Sigurd and the Dragon

Not all important tales in mythology relate to Odin or, indeed, the gods themselves directly. The tale of Sigurd is one such myth, which is of particular relevance to the Norse Tradition.

Sigurd was the son of Sigmund and Hiordis. He was born after his father's death at the hands of a disguised Odin who, having already killed Sigmund, shattered the fallen hero's sword to pieces. Hiordis would go on to bear her late husband's son, giving him the pieces of the sword his father had once carried.

Sigurd, often held to be a distant descendant of Odin, would be raised—partially by his mother and her new husband, the king Alf, but largely by Regin, who became his foster-father. It was Regin who would reforge the sword of Sigurd's fallen father, Sigmund.

Regin had a bit of a complicated history, as he had once been denied his share of gold at the killing of the dwarf, Ótr (also Otr, Ottar, Otter,) his brother. One day, while Otr was swimming in a pool at the base of a waterfall with the dwarf Andvari. In order to do this without her being any the wiser, Otr would don the form of, you guessed it, an otter.

One day, Otr was swimming in the pool when Loki (you just know something bad is about to happen) spotted the creature and, not knowing that the otter was actually Otr in disguise, slayed him. Loki went to show his prize to the king of the dwarves, Hreidmar. Unbeknownst to Loki, Hreidmar was the father of Otr, Regin and Fafnir (more on him in a minute.) The two brothers detained Loki, demanding recompense for their slain brother.

Loki, never one to pay his debts honestly, captured Andvari, the dwarf, and demanded her gold. This she gave, but among the bullion was a ring[18] that would bring dire misfortune to any who wore it. Loki brought the treasure to the bereaved brothers and stuffed Otr's body with it before covering the same with the rest of the gold. He left the ring atop the pile. Shortly thereafter, though, Fafnir killed his father and cut his brother out of his share of the gold.

Back to Sigurd: Regin approached Sigurd one day, telling him that he needed to choose a horse for himself. Sigurd set out to do this and, fortuitously, came across Odin on his way, the latter, in disguise. Odin divined the young man's purpose and told him that the best way to choose his horse would be to chase a band of horses into a river, selecting only the one that swam successfully to the other side as his own. Sigurd did this, and this is how he ended up with his

---

[18] See The Ring of the Nibelungen by Wagner.

horse: A direct descendant of Odin's own steed, Sleipnir.

After Sigurd had his steed, Regin approached him again, telling Sigurd about how his brother, Fafnir, had stolen the gold, literally from his dead brother Otr's body. He also informed him that, due to the ring's cursed power, Fafnir had become a dragon, and that the best way to slay him would be to dig a hole, climb into and cover it to lie in wait for Fafnir to come near. Sigurd listened to this advice, and was also counseled by Odin, again disguised, to dig a trench in addition to the hole in order to capture the slain dragon's blood.

Regin went about forging Sigurd a sword, but when the latter went to test the blade by striking the anvil with it, the weapon splintered in his hand. Regin forged another, but this one also cracked. As they say, though, the third time's the charm. Sigurd brought the fragments of his father's sword to Regin, who re-forged it into a working blade, called Gram (alternately, Gramr.) When Sigurd went to test this blade, not the sword, but the anvil split with the blow. He was now ready to do battle.

Sigurd went to the dwelling of Fafnir and made the necessary preparations. Once lying in wait, Sigurd heard the mighty beast approaching and, at just the right moment, he leapt forth, killing Fafnir.

The blood drained into the trenches and Sigurd bathed in it. This gave him the ability to understand the language of the birds[19], which proceeded to warn him that his mentor, Regin, had also been corrupted by the ring and was plotting Sigurd's demise.

When Sigurd returned, gold in tow, he didn't hesitate in killing Regin. While this wouldn't be the end of the ring, it brought the chapter of Regin and Fafnir to a close.

---

[19] Alternately, he consumed Fafnir's heart at this point, which gave him this power.

CHAPTER 18

Central Myths and Legends: Ragnarök

Ragnarök

Though it was debatable whether to include Ragnarök in this chapter, or to place it in Morality, Life &
Death and the Practical Enactment of the Mythos in
Norse Life[20], it is far too crucial to the Norse Tradition
to hold back further.

Ragnarök is, in Norse Tradition, a cataclysmic event
on the level that would have a devastating effect on
all of the nine worlds. Like many mythologies, Ragnarök is prophesied from the beginning. In fact, the
gods—even, perhaps especially, Surtr who was sharp-
ening his doom blade before other gods even came
into being—are, in one way or another, constantly
preparing for this final battle.

As it is prophesized in the Eddas, the pantheon of
Norse gods, jötnar, elves, Valkyries and others even
knew which way the battle would go, who would die

---

[20] Chapter Six

and at whose hands. The main indication that Ragnarök would be imminent was that there would be three winters in a row without summer dividing them. Despite all of this, the beings refused to sit back and let prophecy run its course.

Key Players in Ragnarök: Jörmungandr

Jörmungandr (also Jǫrmungandr or Jormungand) was a giant, four-legged serpent that surrounded the world of Midgard. Often referred to as the Midgard Serpent or the World Serpent, Jörmungandr would play a vital role in the events of Ragnarök.

Jörmungandr was one of the children of Loki by the jötunn Angrboda[21], and was of such massive size that it encircled the world of Midgardr entirely. A sea-serpent, Jörmungandr was so large, in fact, that its mouth closed over its own tail. It was said that when Jörmungandr opened its mouth, so would begin Ragnarök.

Jörmungandr was the arch rival of Thor, who, in an attempt to kill the serpent, lowered a fishing line, hooking Jörmungandr. Thor attempted to raise the creature from its depths, but when the jötunn, Hymir, saw the scene, he severed the line in fear that Thor was unwittingly about to call forth Ragnarök.

This wouldn't be the final conflict between the two, though. During Ragnarök, Jörmungandr would open its mouth, poisoning the sky. During the heat of the battle, Thor would slay the mighty serpent, only to

---

[21] The other two being Hel and Fenrir.

fall dead after taking nine steps, having been poisoned by Jörmungandr.

Key Players in Ragnarök: Fenrir, the Wolf

Fenrir was a great wolf, son of Loki and the jötunn Angrboda. Now, the events of Ragnarok had been foretold, and so the gods were well aware that, unless they could prevent it, Fenrir would come to kill Odin during the final battle.

Although it was also told that Odin's death would be avenged, the gods set out to change the course of destiny. Sadly, this doesn't usually work, even in mythology.

What the gods did was to attempt to raise the wolf, themselves, hopefully persuading him to align himself with them at the coming of Ragnarök. This plan changed, though, when the gods witnessed the incredible rate of growth of the mighty creature. Their next gambit was to bind Fenrir, rendering him harmless to Odin and the other gods.

The gods, knowing that Fenrir wouldn't submit to this measure voluntarily, went to the wolf, telling him that they wanted to play a game—one which would test his strength. Fenrir agreed, and so allowed the gods to chain him up. He quickly burst through the bonds, proud of his might.

The gods tried again, this time, using a heavier chain, but again, Fenrir broke the bonds without much hassle.

It wasn't until the gods implored the dwarves to create the strongest chains ever created that they had a chance to incapacitate their future foe. The chain was very strong, but was also very light, even soft to the touch. Fenrir, sensing that something was off, said that he would only agree to be bound if one of the gods would place his or her hand in his mouth; thus, if the "game" was, indeed a trick, the gods would pay for their treachery.

As this surely meant that someone was going to lose a hand, the gods were hesitant. Tyr[22] (or Týr,) the god of glory, law and justice finally stepped forward, offering his own hand in exchange for the wolf's trust. Once bound, Fenrir struggled against the chains, but was unable to free himself. He bit the hand from Tyr's body, but he was already bound, unable to move or free himself.

The Death of Baldur, and the Coming of Ragnarök

Baldur was the son of Odin and his wife Frigg. A god of wholesomeness and light, Baldur was much beloved among the gods.

---

[22] Tyr's day is now commonly called Tuesday.

Little is known of Loki's motivation, although it is posited that he hated Baldur for his supposed invulnerability (which will be discussed presently,) but what is told in the Tradition is that Loki would have the beloved god killed.

It all started when Baldur had a prophetic dream about some great tragedy which was to befall him. Frightened for his son, Odin swiftly made his way to the land of the dead where dwelled a powerful, but deceased, jötunn seeress named Vafþrúðnir (or Vathruthnir/Vathrudnir.)

Upon Odin's arrival, he took on a disguise, calling himself Gagnráðr, and woke the seeress. Finding the seeress's dwelling festooned with decorations, Odin asked Vathruthnir for what purpose the feast was to be held. She immediately responded that Baldur would be arriving soon. This may not have been too shocking a statement, if it weren't for the fact that the hall was in the land of the dead. The seeress had just confirmed that Odin's son, Baldur, wasn't long for the world of the gods of Asgard. The seeress did tell Odin, though, that Baldur would be resurrected after Ragnarök.

Odin returned to Valhalla, his hall within Asgard (much more on that later,) with the news that Baldur was to be killed, Frigg travelled far and wide, making every living thing take an oath that they would not kill or harm Baldur... Everything, that is, except for

mistletoe, which the goddess saw as being too in-
nocuous a thing to take such an oath. I think we can
see where this is going.

The gods rejoiced in Baldur's new imperviousness to
harm. They even went so far as to entertain themselves by hurling objects at the god, and watching
them fall away, leaving Baldur completely unfazed.

Loki, upon seeing this, was overcome with a fit of
jealousy. He disguised himself and went before Frigg,
asking her if she had actually convinced every living
thing to take the oath not to harm her son. Frigg
proudly stated that she had, with the exception of
mistletoe, as it was too small and pure to hurt anyone. That was the nail in Baldur's proverbial coffin.

Now armed with the information that mistletoe was
the only substance which could possibly cause Baldur
harm, Loki collected an amount of it and made a
spear from it. He then returned to Asgard, spear in
hand, and approached Hod, the blind brother of Baldur.

Although by accident on the part of Hod, the spear
was thrust into Baldur's body, killing him. The gods
were shocked. Odin and the jötunn conceived and
bore Váli, who grew to full measure within a day of
his birth. Once Váli was at full strength, he killed
Hod.

Baldur was interned by being set upon a funeral pyre, borne upon a ship. The pyre was set aflame, but Baldur wouldn't be the only one upon it, as his wife, Nanna threw herself into the flames[23].

Loki's treachery wasn't over, though. Frigg sent Hermud to try and strike a bargain with Hel to release Baldur from the realm of the dead. Hel, who was joined at the time by a rather morose Baldur, said that if the dead god was so beloved, then every living thing would weep for him, and it was only on the fulfillment of this condition that Hel would agree to return Baldur to Asgard.

The message went out to every creature in all of the worlds, and all wept at the loss of Baldur. All, that is, but Loki, disguised as the jötunn, Thökk (Þökk in the Old Norse.) Having failed, by virtue of Loki's continued duplicity, Baldur was doomed to remain in Hel, with Hel, until after Ragnarök, when he would be resurrected to rule over all. With Baldur's death, and the gods' failure to retrieve him from Hel, the first step in the prophecy of Ragnarök had been fulfilled.

---

[23] Alternately, she died of grief and was then set upon the pyre with her husband.

The Binding of Loki, The Final Battle and the Next Beginning

Loki, having finally been discovered for his part in the scheme, fled Asgard. In order to evade his would-be captors, Loki went to the pool at the base of a waterfall and, having turned himself into a salmon, swam within the stream.

As he emerged in order to fashion a net—in order to capture food—by the light of a fire, Odin, though only one-eyed, spotted him in the distance. Loki divined that the Aesir gods were on his trail, and so he leapt back into the water as a salmon, having cast his net into the fire.

Upon finding the fire, and in it, the net, the gods fashioned their own net to catch Loki. He successfully evaded them, time and time again, but was finally caught by Thor as the former leapt from the water, trying to escape.

Now in the gods' hands, Loki was bound with the entrails of his son, Nari, who had been slain by his other son, Narfi[24] who had been transformed into a wolf. The entrails were turned to iron by the gods,

---

[24] In some tellings, Nari and Narfi are the same being, and the one who was transformed into the wolf was his son, Váli; not to be confused with Odin's son of the same name.

but that wasn't enough punishment for the one who had slain Baldur and, quite literally, brought about the Norse apocalypse. Above his head was hung a venomous snake which dripped poison onto the bound god's face.

With Loki and Fenrir both bound, the gods enjoyed a moment of relief, but Ragnarök was already on its way.

Three roosters crowed[25]: One in the forest Gálgviðr, located in Jötunheim, one in Asgard and the last in Hel. Heimdall, keeper of the Gjallarhorn, an instrument whose sole purpose was to announce the onset of Ragnarök, raised the instrument and sounded the alarm. The world tree, Yggdrasil quaked, and Jörmungandr thrashed, his enormity causing enormous waves to rise and crash.

Surtr came from the south, wielding his sword, and the jötnar advanced on Asgard. The Valkyries—whose job it was to select the bravest of the fallen warriors of humanity, one half of which dwell in a state of constant battle in Valhalla, preparing for Ragnarök[26]—prepared for the onslaught of the jötnar. Meanwhile, the people of Midgard grew ever more destructive toward one another. Perhaps worst of all

---

[25] See the denial of Christ by Peter.

[26] The other half of the honored dead being led to Freyja. More on this in chapter six.

(with the exception of Surtr's presence,) Loki and Fenrir broke free of their bonds, the former leading the charge against the Aesirs aboard the ship of the dead. The sky went dark, as the stars disappeared, and Fenrir ran with his lower jaw dragging the ground, his upper jaw above the sky, consuming everything in his path, including the sun and the moon.

The battle was joined, and Odin was almost immediately consumed by Fenrir, as was Tyr. As foretold, Vidar avenged his father's death by taking the wolf by the jaws and hyper-extending to the point of breakage, finally stabbing the great wolf through the heart.

Freyr and Surtr joined battle with one another, with the bout ending in both of their deaths. Also, Loki met his end at the hands of Heimdall, but not before the former had inflicted a mortal wound upon the latter; thus, they too, killed each other.

Jörmungandr, having released his own tail, rose to Asgard, his mouth open as he unleashed his venom into the air. Thor would kill the serpent, but not before being poisoned himself. He, too, fell dead.

As most of the gods lay dead, the nine worlds sank once more into the water and the nothingness of Ginnungagap reigned once more. Unlike many end-of-times myths, though, the worlds would not be lost forever.

In time, all was recreated with Baldur in charge. All became green and full of life as before. Humanity, which had nearly been eliminated entirely, would be reborn with Lifthrasir and Lif, this time playing the role that Askr and Embla had once played after the first creation of the cosmos. The sun and moon, now the descendants of their predecessors returned to the sky, and all was made new once more.

CHAPTER 19

Morality, Life and Death

Morality to the Norse was, in many ways, akin to those of other polytheistic religions, specifically that of the Greeks and the Romans. Rather than the ascetic nature of the monotheistic religion(s), the gods of the Norse espoused things found in nature. They, like the people who revered them, were often flawed. They could be quick to anger, or to cheat or to deceive or kill. But even those more insidious gods, such as Loki, had their shining moments.

The Norse viewed everything in nature as being attributed to one god or another; or at least some other being or type of being, such as the dwarves or the elves, etc. When a storm rolled in, it was viewed as being Thor's hammer crashing down. Therefore, while the Norse strived to be worthy of Valhalla or the fields of Freyja, they recognized that they, like the gods they revered, were imperfect.

One of the chief ways that the Norse believed they could become worthy of life in Odin's Valhalla or

Freyja's Fólkvangr, was through courage in the face of an enemy, or kindness in the presence of a friend.

While much of the cycles of life and death have already been discussed, there is plenty more to know.

Now, we've established that Hel was the destination for most mortals, those who had brought dishonor upon themselves in one way or another; often through cowardice, treason or otherwise failing or harming their communities and each other.

The honored dead, however, had a much different future ahead of them. The honored dead who fell in battle were led by the Valkyries to Valhalla, or to Fólkvangr, where they would prepare, as their comrades under Odin's watch, for Ragnarök.

It's been stated that the honored dead would do battle in their preparation, and it's important to note that these battles weren't simple training exercises. Those doing battle were the Berserkers, warriors whose skill and fury in battle was unlike anything else on any of the worlds. Those who were bested in Valhalla were killed, just as if they were fighting a true war with one another. After the daily battle, those who had fallen would rise again, and all would come together to drink of mead and feast in each other's company.

Descriptions of Fólkvangr aren't as numerous or as detailed as those of Valhalla, but it's been postulated that the two destinations were of roughly the same nature. Freyja's half of the honored dead would also prepare for Ragnarök as an army; although, while Valhalla was generally the destination of men who had died on the battlefield, Fólkvangr also housed those of honor who were not warriors. Women, men and children could be found in Fólkvangr, but again, not much else is known about Freyja's army.

In their everyday life, the Norse held tightly to family bonds and the bonds with those of their communities with personal responsibility being at the forefront of their minds. This isn't to say that the Norse were a particularly peaceful people.

Vikings, as we know, were generally plunderers, at times conquering lands as far south as France and Spain. Those who stayed in their newly conquered lands, though, generally assimilated rather quickly into the general populous of their new surroundings.

Conquering or sacking the lands of foreigners was considered to be not only a way to prove one's honor and skill in battle, but as a way to strengthen and assert the Norse way of life. Though the Norse didn't believe in killing for the sake of killing, they did believe that if they killed or died in furtherance of strengthening their people, they would be greatly rewarded in the afterlife.

One of the chief reasons for this, and behind much of Norse morality, was how one's actions may influence Ragnarök. It could be said that while the honorable dead would strengthen the gods, therefore, perhaps, giving mankind and its deities a crucial edge in Ragnarök, cowards and criminals would do just as much damage as their cohorts did good.

Hel, despite its modern usage, was to the Norse, not a place of eternal damnation and punishment, but simply as a place where there really wasn't much going on. Furthermore, those who came to dwell in Hel would likely play a small roll (if any role at all) in the events of Ragnarök.

Social ties were viewed as crucial, as those who sought to individuate themselves from their tribes or communities would also end up on their own in the afterlife; specifically, a whole lot of time with Hel.

The concepts of Niflheim and Muspelheim were likely simple allegories to locations, though nonspecific, in nature. To the north of the Norse lands was coldness and barrenness attributed to Niflheim. To the south was the land of heat and fire, attributed to Muspelheim. Put simply, due to the Norse lands' location in the upper part of the northern hemisphere, (Norway, Finland, Denmark, Sweden, Iceland and Greenland,) the Vikings recognized that the more north they went, the colder the land was; the further south they went, the warmer.

The Norse, though devotees of their gods, believed just as strongly in the importance of family and societal ties; what every Viking desired from battle was either a valiant death, or a great victory in which their fellows would all reap the benefit.

CHAPTER 20

From Chosen Tradition to Conversion

This is a small chapter, but it's crucial in Norse history, as it spelled the end for much of the Vikings' ability to hold their chosen religious beliefs. In this chapter, it's not my aim to say that one or the other religion is right or wrong, as that's a personal decision, all for themselves and it's certainly not my place, my goal or my business what anyone else believes. It is, however, useful to give a history of what happened and how.

Early attempts by the Catholic Church (mainly in the eighth and ninth centuries) to convert those in modern-day Scandinavia were largely unsuccessful. Though a few baptisms were performed, and the Catholics did set up some churches, headed by representative leaders among the religion of the time, many among the Norse simply didn't want to give up their traditional beliefs.

In Denmark, where the Vikings were more commonly ruled by local chieftains than by farther reaching authorities, there was a particularly strong antipathy toward Christianity. While raiding in Christian lands, many, though not all, of the individual Viking tribes would bring back Christian slaves or, in some cases, wives—also, assumedly under similar duress as the slaves—as trophies of their conquest.

Those who did convert to Christianity early on often held their traditional beliefs as well, not wanting to offend their old gods and local spirits. The first major converts, such as the Danish King, Harald Klak, did so in order to win favor, and thus, support from the Christian armies or political arms.

Others converted through trickery, such as Harald "Bluetooth" (Blåtand) Gormsson. Gormsson, who, though he had remained pagan for much of his rule had allowed missionaries in his lands, finally converted after a monk held a hot piece of iron in his hand without sustaining injury. This move was also politically motivated, though, as he sought the support of the church's armies in defending his homeland from Germany.

In Norway, when early attempts at conversion failed, Harald Greyhide set about sacking Viking temples and holy sites. This, unsurprisingly, didn't go over too well with the Norse.

While the individual reasons for conversion varied, early on at least, very few are thought to have converted due to a change in faith. Those who were not in positions of political power often converted in order to obtain the fine gifts which the missionaries brought them or, in some cases, to escape the threat of death had they not converted. Even those of higher station in the Viking lands were enamored at the immense wealth of the church, sometimes converting to get a piece of the pie for themselves.

Over time, though, much of the formerly Norse lands converted to Christianity. Some peoples held out against the church, such as the people of Greenland and the Samis in Norway and Sweden who didn't convert en masse until the early 1800s.

Even after the conversion of large populations within the Scandinavian countries, though, many of the people continued to practice their Tradition, though they had to do so in secret.

In time, the formerly Norse lands would join the Christian ranks, even sending many of their warriors to participate in the Crusades. For a time, Christianity was the predominant religion claimed by the peoples of Scandinavia.

Fast-forward to the present day. While much of Scandinavia remains Christians, countries such as Sweden and Denmark have become increasingly secular, even to the point of being among the most secular societies in the world today. Some areas throughout the Scandinavian world hold a great amount of anger toward Christian establishments for what they view as the destruction of their original and chosen culture.

What the future may hold for Christianity in Scandinavia is uncertain and up for debate, but many of these formerly Viking peoples have returned to forms of their earlier beliefs.

CONCLUSION

We've travelled far and wide, uncovering some of the tales and triumphs of the Norse Tradition. While there will always be more to discover, I hope that you have found this text both informative and enjoyable.

If you would like to learn more about the Norse Tradition, I highly suggest picking up a copy of the Poetic Edda. It's the closest we have to a primary source on Norse mythology, written by the Norse themselves. The Prose Edda is also a valuable source. Although it may not have the same veracity as the Poetic Edda, it does have some valuable insight into this compelling Tradition of beliefs.

Although the worlds may have met their demise, just like the Norse Tradition itself, that is a long way from being the end of the story. Mythologies, like civilizations, may rise and fall, but what they leave behind tells us not only of a distant past populated with strange people whose beliefs differ from our own, but gives us all an insight into the world in which we live today. Although the Norse Tradition was almost exclusively practiced in Scandinavia, its residue can now be found worldwide, and its stories have inspired many modern tales of life and death, courage and disgrace.

So, whether you're reading this as an informational overview, or for entertainment, I hope that you've found something to strike your fancy and whet your appetite for history. I use the term history there purposefully, not to imply that these gods and myths were actual events, but in the way that these same influenced countless generations of Norse peoples and continues to do so today.

It has been my honor and privilege to bring you this brief glimpse into the fantastical world of Norse mythology, and I hope that you have enjoyed reading it. Check out the other books in this series, including: Discovering Ancient Egypt, Discovering Ancient Egyptian Mythology, Discovering Ancient Greece and Discovering Ancient Greek Mythology.

The ways of the Vikings will live on to inspire people the whole world over in stories, entertainment and academia. What I love most about history and the mythologies of different peoples is that, regardless how those societies and cultures may different from our own, wherever we may live, our truth and heritage can be found therein. The world over and throughout history, people are people. While we often differ in our belief systems, our politics or even our general approaches to life, there is a common thread throughout. We can always learn from the past and from each other, and I hope we do.

It has been an utter joy to share some of the fascinating world of the Norse with you. I wish you happy reading, and a continued thirst for history!

A Preview of
Martin R. Phillips'
Latest Book

ANCIENT ROME

Rome. Where does one even begin?

Yes, beginning at the beginning is usually the way to go, but with Rome, there were always new beginnings.

From the first king of a then inconsequential settlement to the most powerful of the Caesars, Roman history has inspired and fascinated every generation since its inception.

If you've read the other books in this series, you may notice something different at the outset: This text is much longer. While Egypt ruled for a greater amount of time than Rome, its records aren't as extant as that of the latter. While Greece would go to inspire and even become a portion of the Roman way of life, it was Rome that conquered. Put simply, there are so many sources, from Gaius Suetonius Tranquillus, most famous for his "Lives of the Twelve Caesars," to the senator and historian Tacitus, from Titus Livius Patavinus's "Ab Urbe Condita Libri" ("Books Since the City's Founding,") to Lucius Cassius Dio who wrote his histories in Greek, that it's clear: the Romans knew that theirs was a special culture.

That's not to say that Rome was without its troubles. There were constant wars, even among the Romans themselves. Slavery was common and Rome saw its share of megalomaniacal rulers. Through civil unrest and invasion, Rome's landscape would change frequently throughout its existence.

This book focuses on the period beginning with the founding of Rome to the fall of the Western Empire. Care has been taken to include as much relevant history as possible within the space of this book, but with Rome, there is always more to know. With so many events shaping Rome, its people and its influence, it's difficult not to want to include everything ever written about this great civilization, however impractical it may be. What this text has become is much larger than how it begun and I hope you find within these pages knowledge and intrigue, love, wisdom and capricious folly. There was certainly more than enough of these in Rome…

PS. If you enjoyed this book, please help me out by kindly leaving a review!

Printed in Great Britain
by Amazon